AF607257

Travels to the Otherworld and other Fantastic Realms

"The authors provide a succinct and readable compendium of unexpected journeys from this world to those which lie just beyond our ordinary human experience, as recounted in several ancient and medieval sources: Greek, Latin, Arabic, Scots, Old Czech, and Middle High German. Some of these unknown lands are deep within the forest or over the horizon; others are above or below or *within* our terrestrial world—a parallel universe in a different dimension of space and time altogether but not inaccessible to bold adventurers or curious readers who often discover their real selves in these imagined realms."

Craig R. Davis, professor of English language and literature, medieval studies, and world literatures at Smith College, Northampton, Massachusetts

TRAVELS to the OTHERWORLD and other FANTASTIC REALMS

Medieval Journeys into the Beyond

INTRODUCED AND EDITED BY
CLAUDE AND CORINNE LECOUTEUX

Translated by Jon E. Graham

Inner Traditions
Rochester, Vermont

Inner Traditions
One Park Street
Rochester, Vermont 05767
www.InnerTraditions.com

Text stock is SFI certified

Originally published in French under the title *Voyages dans l'au-delà et aventures extraordinaires: Contes et récits du Moyen Âge* by Éditions Imago
First U.S. edition published in 2020 by Inner Traditions

Cataloging-in-Publication Data for this title is available from the Library of Congress

ISBN 978-1-62055-942-0 (print)
ISBN 978-1-62055-943-7 (ebook)

Printed and bound in the United States by Lake Book Manufacturing, Inc.
The text stock is SFI certified. The Sustainable Forestry Initiative® program promotes sustainable forest management.

10 9 8 7 6 5 4 3 2 1

Text design and layout by Debbie Glogover
This book was typeset in Garamond Premier Pro with Heirloom Artcraft, Parapet, Arlington, Gill Sans MT Pro and ITC Avant Garde Gothic Std used as display typefaces

Contents

part two
Romances of Adventure

introduction
Between the Worlds

Heading off to discover unknown lands—whether for the purpose of conquering them, or to establish new trading outposts, or simply for the sake of advancing knowledge by pressing into the farthest reaches of the world—was always a risky venture during the Middle Ages. If we can believe what the written accounts tell us, there were countless dangers lying in wait for the traveler: overland routes offered almost insurmountable obstacles, near invisible paths, steep mountains, hostile natives, meteors, wild beasts, and reptiles like the *iaculus,* a snake that fell upon its victim from the treetops with the speed of an arrow.

But do not think that sailing the seas was any easier: the blue-green waves contained a host of sea monsters ever ready to attack ships, such as the sawfish, who would unfurl his feathers and raise his tail above the waters and, by means of this improvised sail, set off in pursuit of the vessel and try to stop it. It was also necessary to contend with the currents that would carry you to the Magnetic Mountain or into the jaws of chaos,[1] into which all the oceans spill, along with reefs, sirens, and undines. These perils were echoed in hundreds of legends.

The period of the Middle Ages was like a crucible, in which were melted narrative traditions coming from the four corners of the then known world. It was a time of explorations and discoveries made specifically by travelers, an era during which epics and romances drew a number of themes and motifs[2] from tales and legends, a time in which authors tapped deep into geographies, encyclopedias, travel accounts, bestiaries, and herbals for material with which to spice up their stories. This is one of the ways in which many monstrous men and animals found a place in the writings intended to amaze and delight the readers of that time. Let us look at what one of these cosmographies—dating from 1190—tells us. It is a dialogue in which a teacher answers his student's questions about India:

> In this same country lives the animal called the *cale* [*yale*]: its chest is that of a wild boar, its tail is that of an elephant. He has two horns, each of which measures a *klafter** in length; when the beast wishes to fight, it retracts one horn and fights with the other. When the first horn becomes weary, it retracts it and resumes the fight with the other one. This animal fears nothing as much as black peacocks and is equally bold on water and on land. Also in this country there live yellow bulls who grunt like wild boars, and their faces are split from ear to ear. They also fight with their horns like the previous animal. There is a beast there known as the *manticorti* [manticore]: its head resembles that of a man, but its teeth and the rest of its body are like a lion, and it has the blood-red tail of a scorpion. Its voice sounds like the hiss of a serpent. It runs faster than a bird can fly and eats nothing but human flesh. The *monocerroz* [unicorn] is also there, who is built like a horse but has the head of a stag, the feet of an elephant, and the tail of a pig. He has but one horn that measures some four ells† in length and is as sharp as a razor. This is a terrifying animal. He transfixes everything he meets with his horn, whether it is by the shores of the sea or by the many rivers in which live eels that are thirty feet long.[3]

*[A unit of measure equivalent to a fathom (ca. six feet). —*Ed.*]

†[An ancient unit of measure based on the forearm (ca. 45 inches). —*Ed.*]

To come alive, the stories need heroes whose epic deeds—real or legendary—have left their mark in human memory. While some of these figures like King Arthur, Roland, Siegfried, and Melusine have survived in popular consciousness, how many others are no longer remembered at all today! This book will allow you, the reader, to make their acquaintance.

Travelers' tales open up an unusual world for us; they allow us to discover a mythic geography and meet people from the far ends of the earth. In its own way, each tale reflects the reactions of the human being when faced with the unknown. The letters of Alexander of Macedonia to his mother Olympias and his teacher Aristotle are a perfect example of this. Out of these letters emerge alarming creatures of unparalleled strangeness.

But journeys did not only take place in this world. In the Middle Ages, with its profound Christian imprint, the protagonists could also make their way into the Otherworld, the land of Faery; this is the case with Thomas of Erceldoune [also known as Thomas the Rhymer] or Guerrin Meschino.

The story of the knight Tundale serves as a paradigm here. Having fallen into a coma, the spirit of this knight was stolen away to visit hell and purgatory with an angel as his guide, before finally seeing heaven or its antechamber in the distance. This journey sometimes unfolds *in corpore* by means of a double persona that a deep coma can create, but the clergy preferred to substitute a more orthodox voyage *in spiritu* for this physical journey. In our day, this kind of journey has inspired many authors, such as the French novelists Bernard Werber[4] or Laurent Gaudé.[5] The traveler may also find himself in a place "between the worlds," like Vollarc, who was given lodging there by the devil.

Romances of adventure often resemble travel narratives and follow a similar narrative outline, but the motivation for the hero's departure is not necessarily a desire to discover the world. The story of Duke Ernst gives us an outlaw who sets sail for the Holy Land and is carried off by a tempest into the unknown. The story of Solomon and Marcolf, the first picaresque novel of the Middle Ages, features a man setting off for the East in order to bring back the fickle wife of his king, and the tale of Štilfríd and Bruncvík transports us into an unknown world where individuals are saddled with some peculiar patronyms, such as the king named Astronomus, and another named Olibrius.

In the tales we have brought together here, the element of the "marvelous" (*merveilleux*) or the "world of wonders" is omnipresent. In these stories we meet with fantastic creatures such as bird-men with the heads and necks of cranes, magical objects, potions, trees that can talk, hideous demons inflicting terrible tortures, monsters of all kinds, temporary metamorphoses, seductive fairies, parallel worlds that can often be quite easily entered, and islands inhabited by strange creatures. This is but a sampling of what one may encounter through these narratives.

We have envisioned this book as an introduction to the geography of a wondrous universe by favoring narratives that carry us off into a legendary Otherworld that reflects the dreams and beliefs of an earlier period.

We have given particular attention to the illustrations of the manuscripts and incunabula because they show again and again what their audience found most striking, and what was deemed most worthy of being painted, drawn, or engraved—which is to say, put within reach of the illiterate—as was similarly the case with sculptures and frescoes in the churches. For example, the frescoes at the Albi Cathedral in southern France corroborate what we are told in the story of the knight Tundale, while a sculpture in Remagen, Germany, contributes to disseminating the legend of Alexander the Great's ability to fly through the air. Furthermore, the images are an interpretation of the text—and sometimes are even at odds with it, as the artists allow their imaginations free rein in attempting to depict such remarkable beings. Later, the printing press would help ensure the circulation of the stories and enable the rise of folk literature in the form of chapbooks, even if the latter are often much cruder than the paintings in the manuscripts. The reader will find a good example of this with the story of Solomon and Marcolf.

Signs

🕮 indicates the source of the narrative

🕮🕮 provides bibliographical references for further reading

Motif: refers to the Aarne-Thompson Index (AT) of folktale types

In the notes, when “cf.” appears before an AT motif, this is to indicate a possible kinship between the motif in the story and the one listed in Aarne-Thompson.

part one

Extraordinary Journeys

one

Journeys to the Borderlands

1. ALEXANDER'S LETTER TO OLYMPIAS (GREEK)

After he had defeated Darius and conquered the kingdom of Ariobarzanes and Manazakes,† subjugated Media and Armenia, and the whole of Persia, Alexander set off toward the north.*

King Alexander sends his greetings to his very dear mother and to his teacher Aristotle [. . .]

I brought guides because I wished to push through the desert toward the Plough.‡ They advised me against this course because of the wild beasts living there, but I ignored them. We came to a region with many ravines, where the road was narrow and steep-sided, and for eight days we encountered strange and unknown animals.

We finally entered a large forest of trees called *anaphanta,* which produced a most peculiar fruit: enormous apples as large as gourds. The

*Αριοβαρζάνης was a Persian satrap.

†Manazakes is probably Mazaios (Μαζαῖος), whom Alexander named satrap of Babylon after the Battle of Gaugamela [or Battle of Arbela —*Trans.*] (331 BCE), in the north of what is now Iraq.

‡The Big Dipper.

inhabitants, the Phytoi, a people some twenty-four ells in height, had horns that were around one and one-half ells and had long feet. But their forearms were saws. When they caught sight of us, they rushed to meet us. Horrified at their appearance, I ordered that one be captured. When we attacked them while shouting and blowing the trumpets, they fled. We killed thirty-two of them while one hundred of our soldiers were slain. We remained there for a time to eat the fruits of the anaphanta.

We resumed our journey in a dreary land inhabited by people like giants,[1] who were massive and ruddy like lions. Near them lived the Ochlites, bald men about four ells in height and as wide as a spear. They wore lion hides and were quite skilled fighters. We attacked them but they slew many of us with their clubs. I grew scared and commanded that the forest be set alight. They turned tail once they saw the flames, but only after they had already killed one hundred eighty soldiers.

The next day I decided to visit their caves. We found wild beasts who had three eyes and resembled lions chained in front of the gates. We could see fleas the size of frogs jumping around. We resumed our journey and found a spring, nearby to which I ordered our tents to be set up. We stayed in this place for two months.

We then headed off again and arrived at the land of the Melophagi.* We saw a man who was entirely covered in hair and who was so large he scared us. I ordered him captured, then I had a naked woman go up to him; he seized her and began devouring her.[2] My soldiers rushed upon him to pull her away, but he howled in his incomprehensible language, rousing his companions, around ten thousand of whom came out of the swamp. There were forty thousand of us and, following them in pursuit, we managed to capture three. But they refused all food and died eight days later. They were not human and barked like dogs.

Continuing on our route, we reached a river and called a halt. There were trees in the water there that grew from dawn to noon, then shrunk

*Literally, the "apple-eaters."

away to nothing. Their resin was similar to Persian myrrh and smelled wonderful. I ordered some to be cut down so that their resin could be collected with sponges, but my men were whipped by invisible beings when they tried to do so.[3] We could hear the blows and see their victims fall onto their backs, but those who were holding the whips did not show themselves. A voice then rang out, forbidding us to cut down the trees and to collect their sap. "Stop, otherwise your entire army will be struck dumb." I therefore obeyed this command.

We also found black stones in this river; anyone who grabbed hold of one would turn black. There were also reptiles and all kinds of fish that were not cooked by fire but by cold spring water. We learned this when a soldier washed a fish in the spring, put it in a container and saw that it was cooked. There were also birds similar to the birds of our lands living next to the river, but they breathed out flames when they were grabbed.*

We resumed our journey the next day. Our guides told us: "We do not know where we are going. We should turn around in order to avoid entering even more inhospitable regions," but I refused. We encountered many different animals, some with six paws, some with three or five eyes, some who were six ells long, and many others as well. Some of them fled when we came across them; others attacked us.

We then made our way into a sandy country that was inhabited by peaceful beasts resembling wild asses. They were twenty ells long and had six eyes, but could only see with two of them. The soldiers slew several with their bows.

We then arrived at the land of the headless men,[4] who did however possess human speech. They went fishing—their sole food was fish—and brought us some. They were hairy and clothed in animal hides. Some of them gave us mushrooms that weighed twenty-five pounds each. We also saw a countless number of seals crawling on the shore. Our friends invited us to return, which I had no desire to do at all, as I wished to see the ends of the earth.

---

*These are the legendary hercinia birds.

We continued our advance to the sea and no longer saw any birds or animals. All we could see were the earth and sky, not even the sun; we were completely swallowed by shadow. We raised camp at the water's edge for several days. An island could be seen in the middle of the sea, which I wanted to explore. I had a large number of small boats constructed and some thousand men set sail to make the crossing. We could hear human voices coming from the island and proclaiming in Greek:

O son of Philip, child of Egypt,
Your name is already herald of your great deeds:
Your mother named you *Alexander,* and you have *warded off* and
defeated *men* and driven kings from their kingdoms,
But you will soon become an *ex-man**
When *lambda,*† the second letter of your name, has been fulfilled.

We could not see a soul. Several careless soldiers swam to the island to search it for treasure, but the rest of us returned to the campground in fear.

When we got there, we saw a crab as big as a breastplate emerging from the water. Its claws and front pincers each measured six feet in length. We slew it with some difficulty as the iron of our spears could not pierce its shell, and the crab broke them with its pincers. We found seven pearls of incalculable value in its stomach, and I thought they must have been born in the depths of the sea.

I came up with an iron case in which I had placed a huge glass jar that was one and one-half ells thick. It had an opening at the bottom through which a person could stick out his hand. What I really wanted was to dive into the depths so I could discover what was on the floor of this sea. I would do this by proceeding as follows: I would keep the hole closed until I got to the bottom, whereupon I would open it, stick my hand out in

---

*This reflects an etymological interpretation of the name Alexander: *alex-,* "ward off, repel," and *ex-andr-,* "ex-man" (i.e., deceased).

†The Greek letter *lambda* also corresponds to the number 30, the age at which Alexander died according to legend; historically, he died when he was thirty-three.

order to grab some sand, then I would go back in and close the hole back up. I then had an iron chain that was 308 fathoms long, attached to the cage, and gave orders to not pull me back to the surface unless I shook the chain. When all was ready, I got into the barrel that was then sealed with a lead cover. When I had reached a depth of 120 ells, a passing fish gave a slap of its tail to the cage, and I was pulled back up. The same thing happened on my second attempt. But on my third attempt, I went down to a depth of 308 ells and I saw all kinds of fish. One of them, which was monstrous in size, seized the cage in its mouth and dragged me a full nautical mile. Three hundred sixty men were holding the chain on the boat and it dragged all of them to shore where the beast broke the cage open with its teeth and tossed me onto dry land. Half paralyzed with fear and half dead, I got on my knees to thank divine Providence, and said to myself: "Stop trying to do the impossible, Alexander!" I ordered the army to break camp and we took back to the road.

Two days later we came to a country where the sun never shined; it was the Land of the Blessed,[5] which I wished to explore only in the company of my servants. My friend Callisthenes advised me to bring forty companions, one hundred slaves, and one thousand two hundred sturdy soldiers. I left the foot soldiers behind, along with the old men and the women, and left with the young men after I had forbidden the presence of anyone old. Piqued by curiosity, an old man told his two sons, both of whom were brave soldiers: "My children, obey your father and bring me; I will be helpful in this team. When Alexander finds himself at an impasse, he will look for an Elder,[6] and if he finds one in me, you will be honored for that."

"Father, we dread the king's threat: if we disobey him, we will either have to remain here or we will be executed," they responded.

"Cut off my beard and change my appearance! I am going to join you among your fellow soldiers and will aid you when peril threatens."

They then obeyed their father.

After three days' travel, we came to a dark and gloomy land,[7] and could go no farther because the road was impossible; so we set up our tents. The next day, I left with a thousand armed men to learn if this was the end of the earth. We headed toward the right as it was lighter in that direction. We traveled until noon through a rocky region, hollowed out with ravines. I knew what time it was not from reckoning by the sun but by measuring the distance we had gone. I was gripped with fright and we turned back when it seemed no further advance was possible. This time we took the left-hand course where a very dark plain extended to the horizon. I hesitated before entering because my young companions advised me against entering for fear that the horses would become scattered and lose their way. I answered them: "You who are seasoned warriors can see that without wisdom and intelligence bravery is of no worth. If an Elder had come with us, he would have been able to tell us how to enter this land of darkness. Who among you has the courage to return to camp and bring one back? Your reward will be ten pounds of gold." However, he found no volunteer for this task because the road was long and the sky was black.

The old man's sons sought me out. They spoke to me saying: "Lord if you deign to hear us out without becoming angry, we will reveal something to you."[8]

"Tell me what's on your mind! I swear on divine Providence that I will do you no harm."

They spoke to me about their father and went to get him. When I saw him, I greeted him in friendship and asked his counsel. He responded: "King Alexander, you will never see the light again unless you bring mares who have foals to be your steeds. Leave the foals in the camp before you go exploring; the maternal instincts of the mares will bring you safely back."*

I followed his advice and we found one hundred mares who had recently foaled, and I took them with me. In addition, the old man ordered his sons to gather up whatever they found on the ground during their journey and place it in their bags. We set off preceded by one hundred sixty foot soldiers and two hundred horsemen. We traveled some

---

*A method already attested by Herodotus (*Histories,* III, 102,3 and 105,2).

fifteen *schoinos** and found a clear spring filled with sparkling water. The air was aromatic and not as dark. I was hungry and called Andreas, our cook, and asked him to prepare a meal. He took a dried fish and washed it in the water of the spring. It had barely gotten wet when the fish came back to life and escaped from the cook's hands. Andreas was scared and said nothing of this to me. He drew more of the water that he had drunk and kept a little of it in a silver flask. How unfortunate that fate did not allow me to drink from the spring of immortality,[9] the source that gave life back to the dead, which Andreas had discovered.

After we finished our meal, we marched for some one hundred thirty schoinos before coming upon a light that did not emanate from the sun, moon, or stars, and I spied two birds in flight who had human faces.[10] One shouted down to me: "Alexander, why are you entering a land that belongs solely to God? Turn back, you wretch! It is forbidden to tread upon the ground of the Isle of the Blessed. Go back whence you came, and travel the land that has been granted to you and do not draw misfortune down upon you!"

I trembled and hastened to obey this command. The second bird also shouted in Greek: "The East is calling you. You will conquer the kingdom of Poros!" I prayed and then used the mares as our guide as well as the Plough. Our return journey took twenty-one days, the last of which we were accompanied by the whinnying of the foals.

Many of the soldiers had taken everything they had found and the sons of the old man had filled their bags. Once we were free of the darkness, it was seen that what they had brought back was pure gold and priceless pearls. All the soldiers who had only brought back little or nothing at all regretted they had not done likewise, and all praised the old man for his good advice.

After we had returned, Andreas told us what had happened to him at the spring. When I heard his tale, I was overcome with misery and

---

*[An Egyptian unit of measure, which according to Herodotus was equal to 60 stadia. The Egyptian equivalent is assumed to be around 10 kilometers (roughly 6 miles). —*Ed.*]

punished him harshly. I then told myself: "Alexander, it does no good to cry over the past." I did not know that he had drunk the water and had kept some of it, because he only told us about the fish. Andreas made advances to my daughter Unna and seduced her by promising to give her some of the water of life, which he did. When I learned of this, I must confess that I was envious of their immortality. I summoned my daughter and told her: "Take all your things and get out of my sight! You are immortal and have become a demon; you will be known as Nereida because you gained your immortality from the water."[11]

She left me in tears to go live with the demons and no longer with humans. I then ordered a millstone be tied around the neck of Andreas and for him to be cast into the sea; he transformed into a demon[12] and settled in a land beneath the waves that now bears his name.*

All of these events helped me grasp that I had truly reached the edge of the world. I had a gigantic arch erected there, on which these words were inscribed: "You who wish to see the land of the Blessed, go toward the right-hand side to avoid your deaths."

I then began to think on this and again wondered: "Is this truly the edge of the world, the place where heaven meets earth?" Wishing to know the truth of this for certain, I had several of the birds of this land captured.† They were very large and white, and would not flee from our presence.[13] Several soldiers climbed onto their backs and were carried off into the sky.[14] These birds, who fed on carrion, were drawn to our camp to eat our dead horses. I had two of them caged and starved of food for three days. On the third day I ordered the construction of a kind of wooden yoke that was attached to their necks; then I made a kind of basket out of cowhide in which I installed myself. I carried a spear some seven ells in length that had a horse's liver stuck on the tip. The birds soared off at once, trying to catch it, and carried me into the skies with them.[15] We soared so high I believed I was able to touch heaven. The intense cold caused by the

*The story of Andreas is reminiscent of the legend of Glaukos, but in the latter tale it is an herb that gives immortality.

†In fact, these are griffins.

beating of their wings made me shiver. Finally, a winged being who was human in appearance* came to meet me and said: "Alexander, you understand nothing about the earthly realm and you are aspiring to reach the realm of heaven? Quickly return to earth so you do not end up becoming a meal for these birds. Look at the earth below!"

In terror I obeyed and I saw a huge dragon forming a circle, at whose center was a circular space similar to a small threshing floor. The creature spoke again to me: "That is the earth. The serpent surrounding it is the sea. Lower your spear toward it and go back down!" I followed his advice and returned to the earth [at a distance of] a seven-days' march away from my vassals. I made my way back to camp, fully determined to no longer attempt the impossible. May all be well with you.

ΒΙΟΣ ΑΛΕΞΑΝΔΡΟΥ ΤΟΥ ΜΑΚΕΔΟΝΟΣ ΚΑΙ ΠΡΑΞΕΙΣ, BK. II, 27–41.

📖 *Life and Deeds of Alexander of Macedonia,* II, 27–41, in Meusel, ed., *Pseudo-Callisthenes nach der Leidener Handschrift herausgegeben.*

2. DHUL-QARNAYN'S ENTRY INTO DARKNESS NEAR THE NORTH POLE IN SEARCH OF THE SPRING OF LIFE (MEDIEVAL ARABIC)

Several Arab scholars appropriated the legend of Alexander, who was known as Dhul-Qarnayn,† meaning "the Two-Horned One" because he went to the "two horns of the world," in other words, its two ends. Thalabi,[16] referring to the prophet al-Khidr,‡ recounts one of the raids of the Macedonian when he had set off in search of the Water of Life.[17]

*An angel.

†This name also means "He who has the power to rule over the two ends of the earth"; he was given this name by Hizqiyā'il, the guardian angel of Mount Qaf, the mythical mountain that stands at the edge of the world.

‡*Al-Khidr* means "the Green One," because the earth turns green beneath his steps; furthermore, he has power over the four cardinal points, the air, and the sea; he is invisible or visible at will. One legend claims that he is Alexander's first cousin. In the Koran (18:59–81), he accompanies Moses.

Dhul-Qarnayn had conquered all there was to be found between the West and the East. He had a friend among the angels,[18] Raphael, who often visited him. One day while they were conversing, Dhul-Qarnayn asked him: "O Raphael, what is your divine service compared to ours?"

The angel answered him with tears: "There are angels in heaven who are always standing and are not allowed to sit down, or those who bow eternally and have no right to lift their heads, or even those who are bent over and are not permitted to stand back up."

They cry: "Praised be his holiness, the master of angels and the Holy Spirit. O Lord, we do not serve you as you deserve."

Dhul-Qarnayn wept bitter tears and said: "I wish to live eternally so that I might achieve what is worthy of him and his service."

"Is this truly your desire?"

"Yes!"

Raphael said: "God owns a spring on earth that is called the Spring of Life.[19] He has decided that whoever drinks a mouthful of this water shall not die before he prays to his Lord to slay him."

"Do you know where this spring is?"

"No! We tell each other in heaven that God possesses a Darkness[20] on earth that no man or djinn may enter, and we assume the spring is there."

Dhul-Qarnayn gathered together all the scholars in the world as well as all the individuals who knew the Holy Books and prophetic scriptures, and told them: "Teach me if you have discovered in the holy scripture or the tradition of the prophets which have come down to you, that God has placed a spring on earth that is called Spring of Life."

"No," they all replied, save one who spoke up: "I have read in the Testament of Adam that God created a Darkness into which no man and no djinn could enter, and that the spring of immortality is to be found there."

"What part of the world is it in?" asked Dhul-Qarnayn.

"In the one where the horn of the sun is located."

Dhul-Qarnayn gathered together lawyers, noblemen, and kings, then set off for the East. They traveled twelve years before reaching the outskirts of the Darkness, which boiled like steam, and he set up camp. He summoned the scholars and told them: "I wish to enter this Darkness."

"O king," they responded, "the sovereigns and prophets, who have come here before you, made no attempt to visit it—follow their example! We fear that some misfortune will befall you as well as upon the earth and all who dwell on it."*

"I must enter!"

"Please, O king, abstain from this wish! If we knew that God would not be annoyed at seeing you take what you desire, we would definitely follow you, but we are fearful of divine condemnation as well as the end of the world and all its people."

"I must enter!"

"Then, that is your business," they replied.

"What are the animals with the best eyesight at night," asked Dhul-Qarnayn.

"That would be horses."

"And which horses?"

"The mares."

"And which mares?"

"The youngest ones."

Dhul-Qarnayn had six thousand mares chosen for this task, and then selected six thousand courageous and sensible men from his army. He gave each man a horse and gave Khidr the command of a vanguard of two thousand men. He would follow with a force of four thousand men. He then commanded the rest of the army: "Do not leave the camp for twelve years.[21] If we come back here by then, all will be well; if not, return to your homes and household gods."

Khidr then said to the king: "O king, look, we are entering the Darkness without knowing how much time this journey will take and

*It was once believed that the health of a country was dependent upon the health of the sovereign.

without being able to see one another. What will we do if we get lost?"

Dhul-Qarnayn handed him a red stone and told him: "If you become lost, cast this on to the ground. If it makes a noise, those who are lost will walk toward its sound."

Khidr left. While forging ahead he stumbled upon a valley and, following his inspiration, immediately thought that the spring was very likely to be located there. He stopped at the edge and told his companions: "Stay here! Don't stray far from each other." He then cast the stone into the valley and waited a long time. Finally, he heard the stone and, walking in the direction of the noise, discovered it again and found himself on the edge of the spring. He undressed and entered the water. It was whiter than milk and sweeter than honey. He drank and washed, performed his ablutions, and then threw the stone in the direction of his companions. When he found them again, he leaped astride his horse and said to them: "In the name of God, let's get out of here!"

But Dhul-Qarnayn never discovered the spring. He and his men crossed through the Darkness for forty days and forty nights before the sky began to grow lighter, but it was not a light cast by the sun or moon. They reached a land of red sand that crunched underfoot, and then stumbled upon a castle that was as large as a squared *parasang** and equipped with one door. His army set up in front of the castle and he entered alone.

On an iron bar that stretched from one end of the building to the other, he saw a black bird that resembled a lark,[22] who spoke to him: "Dhul-Qarnayn, you have forged your way to this point, but could you not be content with what you have achieved? Climb this stairway and you shall find what you desire."

Dhul-Qarnayn obeyed the bird's command and encountered a youth whose eyes were turned toward heaven with one foot forward and the other one backward. He held his hand in front of his mouth. With an air of disapproval, he addressed Dhul-Qarnayn: "Could you not be

*[An ancient Persian measure of distance, for which classical writers offered varying equivalents. —*Trans.*]

content with what you have already seen from crossing over the sea and through the Darkness back to me?"

"Who are you?" his visitor asked.

"I am the master of the trumpet* and I am awaiting the orders of my Lord."[23]

He then handed him a stone, the secret of which only Khidr could explain.[24]

On the road back, Dhul-Qarnayn reports, we traveled through the dark and entered the Vale of Emeralds. "Gather what you find," Dhul-Qarnayn ordered. "He who only takes some will feel regret as surely as he who takes nothing."

There were those who took, and those who did not, but later, when these objects proved to be emeralds,[25] all felt regret.

This narrative is the work of a certain Thalabi, about whom we know nothing except for the fact that the person he names as his source, Ali Ben Abi Talib, is also unknown to us. The manuscripts that have transmitted the legend date from 1119 and 1497. Another author, named Omara (eleventh–twelfth century), has transmitted a variant of this text. For the great Persian writer Ferdowsi (circa 940–1020), who follows the Syriac version of Pseudo-Callisthenes, the Darkness lies beyond the Land of Darkness. The Copts situate this land in Arabia, speaking of a spring of

*This is thus the angel Israfil, who will announce the end of the world.

water that makes its drinker immortal, located on the right side of the rising sun, and they make Khidr the military general El-Khidr. The poet Nizami (1141–1209) also mentions the legend of a spring of immortality in his Eskander-Nāma, *written around 1203. In his version, it is the prophet Khidr who discovers the spring, which sits beneath the pole, in the Land of Darkness. The stone that Alexander gives him is a carbuncle, which lights up when it is in close proximity to the water of life. The spring disappears when Khidr leaves to join Alexander again, and the prophet realizes that this water was not destined for him.*

📖📖 Budge, *The Life and Exploits of Alexander the Great,* 246–47 and 261–72; Ethé, "Alexanders Zug zum Lebensquell im Land der Finsternis" (text of Nizami's *Eskandar-Nāma* [1194–1200] with translation and commentary); Kappler, "Métamorphoses alchimiques de la mort en littérature persane Classique"; Lévi, "La légende d'Alexandre dans le Talmud" and "La légende d'Alexandre dans le Talmud et le Midrasch"; Lidzbarski, "Wer ist Chadhir?"; Wünsche, "Alexanders Zug nach dem Lebensquell."

3. ALEXANDER'S LETTER TO ARISTOTLE (LATIN)

Even in the midst of the great dangers and difficulties of our campaign, I have continued to think about you who, after my mother and sister, are the one I love best, and as I know you live for the sciences, I thought it would be a good idea to inform you about the lands of India, about its climate, its countless species of snakes, men, and wild beasts, so that your own knowledge will be enriched [. . .]. It is astounding to see what the earth produces as both good and evil, plants, stones, and living things, and they are so numerous that man does not have enough names to name them all.

I am going to speak of what I've seen and strive not to be accused of fairy tales and lies [. . .].

We set up camp near a river. At the eleventh hour of the day, we sounded the trumpets. I ate and ordered my soldiers to do the same. The first rays of moonlight brought a countless number of scorpions, with tails raised, to our camp. They were followed by a numberless horde of vipers and cerastes.* Some had red scales, others were black and white, and yet others shined like gold. Hissing sounds surrounded us, and our fear was great. We sealed off the camp with our shields and used our spears to stab these wicked monsters, which took two hours until they flowed back the way they came in defeat.

Further on, we came to a lake girded by a thick forest. We slaked our thirst and raised camp after unloading the sumpters,† and then we lit five hundred fires, for there was an abundance of wood. In the third hour of the evening, when we were hoping to get some sleep, two- and three-headed serpents appeared to slake their thirst. They had crests as large as columns. They lifted their heads and darted their forked tongues from their wide-open mouths, their eyes shone with venom and their breath was fatal. We fought against them and lost thirty slaves and twenty soldiers.

Then came a host of crayfish with the hides of crocodiles that resisted our spears. Many of them perished in our fires while others made their way back into the water.

We had not yet been sleeping very long when the trumpets sounded the extinguishing of the fires, but white lions the size of bulls with upraised manes besieged us with extraordinary roars. They hurled themselves upon our spears causing huge chaos that was made even worse by the darkness. Monstrous boars then showed up with bristles that stood up like fence posts, and among them we saw spotted foxes, tigers, and terrible panthers. This was followed by an invasion of mice that were as big as pigeons and had human teeth, which they used to tear my soldiers to pieces. A monstrous beast then appeared; it was the size of an elephant but had three horns on its forehead; the Indians call it Odontotyrannus.‡ It was black and had a head that looked like that of a horse. Once it had drunk its fill, it rushed at us undeterred by the

*[Venomous vipers with horns. —*Ed.*]

†Beasts of burden, pack animals.

‡A mythical image of the rhinoceros. Its name means "tooth-tyrant."

flames. I sent a group of Macedonians to oppose it, but it slew thirty-six of them and trampled another fifty-two, making them unfit for combat. We had the greatest difficulty piercing it with our spears.

Just before dawn another horde of monsterlike frogs, who changed colors, penetrated our camp. They were accompanied by mice as big as foxes. The animals that were bitten died on the spot but this was not the case with the men. With the first gleam of dawn, there appeared nycticorax,* birds similar to vultures but much larger and dark yellow in color with black beaks and claws. The entire lakeshore was covered with them, but they were happy to remain there eating fish. We dared not disturb them and waited until they dried their claws and flew away. I then had my men break the arms and legs of our guides who had led us into such an ambush, and they were then left exposed to the elements so they could be eaten alive by the serpents, as they had intended to happen to us—a well-deserved punishment.

After assembling the army and exhorting the soldiers to keep up their courage, we quickly headed south to the sound of trumpets. I waged war with the barbarians and the Indians, entered into Bactria,† and four days later encountered Poros with his army, which I defeated. He led us to the monuments to Hercules and Dionysus at his kingdom's borders; then I wished to know if there were yet more things to be discovered. I had heard about forests and mountains at the side of the ocean inhabited by reptiles and elephants. I decided to go there, if possible by sailing there on the sea that surrounds the land, but I was told that this ocean was dark and full of abysses. Because no one else had ever gone beyond the Pillars of Hercules and Dionysus, I wished to earn renown by going farther than either of them, and we set off.

We came to a dried-up marshland filled with reeds and wished to cross through it, but came upon an unknown two-headed beast with a spine equipped with teeth like sawblades. One of these heads was like

*An imaginary bird whose name literally means "night crow."

†This empire in central Asia covered what are now the countries of Afghanistan, Tajikistan, and Uzbekistan.

that of a lioness and the other was that of a crocodile with sharp teeth. It hurled itself upon us and killed two soldiers. As we could not pierce it with our spears, we slew it using hammers.

Shortly afterward we reached the last Indian forests and set up camp on the edge of the river Buemar. Our foragers and woodsmen returned to the camp in a state of terror and gave the alarm: large herds of elephants were coming out of the woods. I ordered the Thessalian cavalry to mount their horses and to drive our swine before them by striking them ceaselessly and herd them into the monsters. I ordered this as the squealing of the pigs would send the elephants fleeing, which is precisely what happened.[26]

At dawn we continued on our way and crossed through other regions of India. We came upon the fields of men and women who were as furry as wild animals and measured nine feet. They were known as the Ichtyophages as they fed on raw fish.[27] Once they caught sight of us, they dove into the waters of the Ebdimaris. We then entered forests filled with powerful cynocephalic beings.* They tried to attack us but we sent them fleeing with our arrows. Once we had made our way to the gates of the deserts, we returned to Fasiace† because the Indians told us there was nothing left to see.

After traveling around twelve miles, we raised camp near a spring but hardly had our fires been lit when a storm out of the east blew in and carried away our tents. The soldiers were of the belief that the gods were displaying their anger because I had gone beyond the Pillars of Hercules and Dionysus, but I informed them that this was an equinoctial storm that typically occurred in the fall. We settled at a dry spot a little farther away, but once evening fell, a merciless cold accompanied by an enormous snowfall came in. Out of fear of being buried in the snow, everyone trampled on it so that it would quickly melt and free the fires. A sudden downpour caused the snow to vanish and saved us.

*A kind of ape.

†This may be a reference to Prasiake [Prachya], a city in Delhi Province on the banks of the Saraswati (Sarsooty).

Then a black cloud arrived and a number of flaming small clouds could be seen falling from the sky. They could easily have been mistaken for torches. The fire burned the backs of our animals and our soldiers protected themselves with the aid of clothing. Then the sky grew clear. For three days things went on this way, the threatening cloud floated above us, and the sun was veiled. After we buried some five hundred soldiers killed by the snow, we resumed our march.

We also saw the promontories of Ethiopia,* as well as the Nysaean mountains and the cave of Dionysus. We sent some rogues there because it was said a curse would strike any who entered, and that they would die from fever in three days, which proved to be entirely true. Because there was nothing left to see, we took the road back to Fasiace. Previously, we had walked south.

Our path crossed that of two old men and I asked them if they knew of anything interesting in the area. "If you take this path, which is a difficult one because of its lack of water and the many wild beasts there," they answered, "you will see things that are incredible: the trees of the Sun and the Moon. They speak Indian and Greek.[28] The first is male and the second female. They will tell you what lies in store for you, both good and bad."

I thought they were making fun of me, and I confronted them with the threat of punishment, but they swore they were speaking the truth. So I took forty thousand young and robust men, as well as the cavalry, and sent the rest of the army back to Fasiace. I followed the two old men who led us all the way to the sanctuary. The high priest was a black-skinned man who was more than seven feet tall and had the teeth of a dog. Pearls hung from his pierced ears, and he was clad in animal hides. He asked us: "What have you come here for?"

"I wish to see the trees of the Sun and the Moon," I answered. "If you have not had congress with a woman or child, you may enter the

*According to geographical notions of the time, this country was thought to be located next to India.

sacred grove," he responded, before ordering my three hundred friends and companions to take off their rings, clothes, and shoes.

Everyone obeyed him out of respect for his religion. At the eleventh hour, the priest was waiting for the sun to set and said: "The tree of the Sun speaks at the rising and the setting of its heavenly body, and the tree of the Moon does the same." I was convinced that he was lying.

I visited the sacred grove. It was encircled by a crude wall and filled with the scents of the balm flowing from the trees. Two trees that looked like cypresses stood at the center of the grove; they measured one hundred feet, and the Indians called them *breboniae.** No rainfall watered them; no wild animal, bird, or reptile ever entered these grounds. When an eclipse of the moon or sun occurred, both trees would stream with tears out of fear for their god. I wanted to offer them a sacrifice, but the high priest dissuaded me and urged me to kneel before them and kiss their trunks.

"Will they answer me in Greek or in Indian?" I asked the priest.

"The tree of the Sun predicts the future in both languages, that of the Moon only in Greek," he answered.

As both their tips were now bathed in the light of the setting sun, he added: "Everyone look up at the sky and each think of what he would like to know, but speak not a word of it to anyone!" We all looked around to see if there was anyone hidden nearby to make fun of us but when we saw nothing of the sort, we all heeded the high priest.

I thought: "Will I ever see my mother Olympias and my dear sisters again, and will I return to my country in triumph after conquering the world?" The tree suddenly responded in Indian with a very gentle voice: "Undefeated in war shall you be, Alexander, and sole master of the world, but you shall never return alive to your home, for destiny has already set the date of your death." Because I did not understand what the tree had told me, I forced the Indian translators with threats to translate the oracle that gave them gifts. This prediction terrified me, and I was vexed

*In the Greek Alexander romance they are called *Moutheamatous,* a compound word making use of the names of the Iranian sun and moon gods, Mithras and Mao.

that I had brought so many companions with me. My friend wept bitterly. I consoled them and commanded them to keep this secret.

I then wished to hear the oracle of the Moon. The priest told me: "Not before midnight, when it rises." I only brought with me my three most faithful friends, Perdicas, Ditoricas, and Philotas, as I feared nothing in this place where it is forbidden to kill. We entered the sacred grove, then I asked the tree of the Moon where I would die. "Alexander," the tree answered when the first ray of the moon touched it, "you have already reached the end of your life. You will die in Babylon in a year and nine months' time, betrayed by someone you least suspect."* My friends and I wept bitter tears, but I was incapable of believing that I was threatened by any crime or felony. We left the grove and I went to get some rest. My companions forced me to eat some food; then I returned to the sacred grove so I could be present there when the sun rose. I woke the high priest up and asked the tree what assassin against whom I should seek to protect myself and what the deaths of my mother and sisters would be. It answered me in Greek: "If I revealed him to you, you could kill him and change fate, then the three sisters Clotho, Lachesis, and Atropos,† would have it in for me. You shall die in one year and nine months in Babylon, not by iron as you fear, nor by gold, silver, or any other metal, but by poison. Your mother will also meet a miserable end and die unburied, prey to birds and wild beasts.‡ Fate wishes long happy lives for your sisters. Although little time remains for you to live, you will be master of the world. Ask no more questions but leave this sacred grove and return to Fasiace!" I kept my silence about the oracle around my men and announced to them that we would be leaving. Out of their loyalty to me, my friends kept the secret.

We came to the Jordan valley, which was the home to reptiles that wore emeralds at their throats, which reflected the gleam of their eyes.[29]

---

*At the instigation of Antipater, the regent of the empire, Alexander's cupbearer Iollas poisoned the great conqueror.

†The three Fates.

‡Olympias was killed on Cassandra's orders in 316.

They dwelled in a ravine that was inaccessible because above it rose pyramids that were thirty-five feet high. The serpents fought against each other once a year, at the beginning of spring, and many would die. We collected several enormous emeralds there.

We were then threatened by animals that were constructed like this: they had the heads of lions, large feet, and a tail endowed with two talons they used to dispatch the men they battled. They were accompanied by griffins that had eagle beaks. They swooped down on our eyes and faces and smashed our shields and bucklers. We slew them with our arrows and spears, but I lost six hundred soldiers that were bitten by these beasts and griffins. We slaughtered around sixteen thousand of them.

Reeds grew at the sides of the Occluadas that were so huge that thirty soldiers could barely manage to carry them. The ground was covered with a thick layer of ivory because millions of elephants lived there. Fortunately, they refrained from attacking us; otherwise we would have been trampled. We crossed this river on rafts made from the reeds and encountered hospitable Indians who offered us red and white sponges, and shells with a capacity of two to three gallons,[30] clothing made from the hides of young sea calves, snails that weighed one pound each, and, thicker than a human thigh, enormous mushrooms,[31] redder than scarlet, and moray eels that weigh two hundred pounds, while swearing to us that even larger ones were to be found in the nearby ocean that was some twenty-three miles away. They also fished for five-hundred-pound sparids in the river, for which they used ivory fish pots so these fish would not be able to tear them to pieces and to also prevent the women with their long hair of wondrous beauty from diving into the water in order to devour them. When strangers were found swimming in the river, they would imprison them in the eddies and drown them, or else they would drag them into the reeds and kill them after their sexual desires had been satisfied. We captured two of them. Their skin was as white as that of a nymph and their hair covered their back.

There were also great curiosities on the banks of the Ganges. So no one will be tempted to consider me a liar, I will only say one thing: the waters of the Ganges and the Euphrates flow from north to south, and both these rivers are so wide that one cannot see either side from the other.

We came to the land of the Seres* who are considered to be the most honest and upright people in the world. It is said that murder, adultery, perjury, or drunkenness never occur in this land. The people there live on bread, vegetables, and water. They gave us a warm welcome and set us on the route that, by way of the Caspian Gates,† led to Fasiace in the land of Poros. Our journey was favored by a good east wind, and we encountered many extraordinary beasts: they had bones on their head that were in the form of saw teeth. They swooped upon us like bulls and slew some 9,450 soldiers. After many indescribable efforts, after knowing fear and confronting a thousand perils, we reached the land of Porus. I then commanded Alcon, the governor I had appointed to oversee Persia, to erect in this land and in Babylon, two massive pillars that were twenty-five feet high, and to have engraved upon them all my exploits. I also commanded that two golden, ten-foot-high pillars be placed for me at the far end of India, beyond those of Hercules and Dionysus. In future centuries, my dear teacher, this will be but a very minor wonder.

Dear Aristotle, with our deeds we have raised a new and lasting monument as a sign of our tireless spirit so that our memory and glory remain living eternally.

Epistola Alexandri ad Aristotelem

📖 Bergmeister, *Die Historia de preliis Alexandri Magni;* Burkhart, *Die äthiopische Alexanderlegende*; Christians, *Die serbische Alexandreis;* Feldbusch, ed., *Der Brief*

*The Chinese.

†Historically speaking, this would be the Sirdarra Pass, the border between Media (between the Caspian Sea and the Persian Gulf) and Hyrcania (the northeastern part of what is now Iran).

Alexanders an Aristoteles über die Wunder Indiens; Hilka, ed., *Der altfranzösische Prosa-Alexanderroman;* Hilka, ed., *Historia Alexandri Magni (Historia de preliis) Rezension J² (Orosius-Rezension);* Raabe, ed., *ιστορία Ἀλεξάνδρου: Die armenische Übersetzung der sagenhaften Alexander-Biographie ("Pseudo-Callisthenes");* Ryssel, "Die syrische Übersetzung des Pseudo-Kallisthenes."

Donath, *Die Alexandersage in Talmud und Midrasch;* Pfister, *Kleine Schriften zum Alexanderroman;* Stoneman, *Legends of Alexander the Great;* Weymann, *Die äthiopischen und arabischen Übersetzungen des Pseudo-Kallisthenes; Lexikon des Mittelalters,* vol. 1, col. 354–66.

4. THE ADVENTURES OF ALEXANDER IN IMAGES

Alexander's legend was so popular that it was translated into all the Western languages as well as those of the Middle East and Persia. A large number of these manuscripts are richly illustrated and essentially depict the most striking scenes of the narrative, especially those in which monsters and other strange creatures appear.

The spread of the legend by means of images was not limited to manuscripts, and the artwork on a number of religious buildings also attests to the story's popularity. Two examples are offered here.

Harley Manuscript 4979, Folio 60 and Those Following

The Cyclops

The Gigantic Wild Man

The Acephalic Men

The Imprisonment of Gog and Magog

Extracts from Various Manuscripts

The Flight of Alexander

Munich Cgm 581, folio 133

Manchester, John Rylands Library,
Arm 3 folio 108

Bodleian Library 265, folio 81

San Donnino de Fidenza Cathedral Emilia Romagna, Italy

Pfarrkirche (Parish Church), Remagen, Germany

The Dive to the Bottom of the Sea

Bodleian Library 264, folio 50

Munich Cgm 581, folio 134

Munich Cgm 336, folio 152

two

Journeys to the Otherworld

1. THE PRINCE IN PARADISE (LATIN)

A Christian king gave a woman in marriage to his only son and wished to celebrate the wedding in a solemn fashion. Before the marriage celebration, the prince left the castle to while away some time. He really wished to invite several poor people to the feast. He saw a poor but noble old man approaching him from afar. He went to meet him, greeted him respectfully, and asked him why he had come. "I came to ask for alms," the old man responded. Full of joy, the prince led him to the castle and sat him down at the banquet table facing him, unable to tear his eyes away from the old man's face. The appearance of the old man's extremely noble face gave him so much pleasure that he forgot the meal, the music, and all other worldly delights. In its stead he preferred staring at this face that seemed more and more admirable to him. Once the meal had ended, the old man thanked him and sought to leave, but the young man begged him to stay. "I have but one desire, to spend the rest of my life close to you." The other declined his offer and told him: "I cannot stay here. If you wish to see me again, at this same time tomorrow I will send you a young donkey that can bring you to me." He then departed, leaving behind a very unhappy young man who gave not a thought to his marriage and could only await the next day with impatience.

And in truth, the next day a donkey without a rider arrived at dawn. The prince mounted on its back and, a short while later, found himself in a land where a gentle breeze was blowing and where stood magnificent thickets full of beautiful flowers and trees where the ravishing songs of birds echoed. He next came to a golden castle adorned with precious stones, in which he could see a multitude of beautiful people. He entered the courtyard and encountered an old man who asked him: "Why have you come here?"

"I was invited by a pauper whom I invited to my wedding feast," the prince responded to this venerable old man.

With a smile, the man replied: "That pauper is the creator of all things, our God." He then grabbed the prince's hand and led him to the dwelling of his lord. When the prince's eyes fell upon him, he recognized him immediately and his heart filled with bliss. The prince had gone so deeply into contemplation of his lord's face, which appeared more and more sublime, he forgot all about the sumptuous feast that had been served to him. He had one sole desire: to stay. "That is not yet possible," the lord replied. "Go back home and one day soon you will return and remain with me for eternity."

Mounted on his donkey, the prince took the road back home in great anguish. When he got there it seemed it should only be noon, but his father's palace lay in ruins, and in its stead stood a monastery. He went inside and found that no one recognized him. When he finally asked for news of his father, the abbot summoned all the monks and asked them to consult all their records. They discovered that the prince had gone missing three hundred years ago.[1] He was brought to the tomb of his parents, and at his request the monks opened the grave of his fiancée. Her body was still whole and unblemished, and her face was as pink as if she were still alive. She opened her arms, the prince went down into her crypt, and she embraced him. This was how he disappeared before the eyes of the monks who had accompanied him there, and entered the kingdom of the Son of the Most Holy Virgin Mary.

De hospitalite et fundatione claustri cluniacensis, siue de nupcys eternis (tenth-century manuscript)[2]

The oldest confirmed version of this story can be found in a sermon by Maurice de Sully (1105/1120–1196) and concerns a monk who let himself be seduced by the secular life outside the monastery.

In one of his sermons preached in the vernacular, the Franciscan Roberto Caracciolo (1425–1495) mentions the death of a monk to whom an angel had revealed the ecstasies of heaven. This narrative (which is the type AT 471 A; Tubach exemplum 3378), can be found in a variety of forms in many countries of Europe.

📖📖 Delarue and Tenèze, *Le Conte populaire français,* IV, 278; *Enzyklopädie des Märchens,* vol. 2, col. 835–38; Hammerich, *Munken og fuglen;* Müller, *Die Legende vom verzückten Mönch;* Robson, *Maurice of Sully and the Medieval Vernacular Homily with the Text of Maurice's French Homilies from a Sens Cathedral Chapter ms.,* 124–27; Röhrich, *Erzählungen des späten Mittelalters und ihr Weiterleben in Literatur und Volksdichtung bis zur Gegenwart,* vol. 1, 124–45 (seventeen variants of the story); Scherf, *Das Märchenlexikon,* I, 394–96.

2. TUNDALE THE KNIGHT (LOW GERMAN)

The Visio Tnugdali [Vision of Tnugdalus, Tondolus, or Tundale] *was written around 1148 in Latin by an Irish monk from Regensburg. It enjoyed considerable popularity, as is shown by the many translations into the common vernacular that exist. It recounts the tribulations of a soul that is traveling the regions of the Otherworld.*

This book tells the story of a knight named Tundale and of his soul that was carried away,[3] which saw so many things: the sufferings of hell and the torments of Purgatory, the joys of eternal bliss, and other wonders.

In the year of Our Lord 1049, the fortieth year of the reign of Pope Eugenius of Iberia, lived a knight named Tundale, who was a native of southern Iberia. He was of noble birth, but was a cruel and handsome man, both proud and strong. He spared little thought to his own salvation and even grew irritated when others spoke to him on this matter. He avoided going to church and to Mass, having no desire to hear or see the poor, and, because of his great vanity, was extremely generous to mountebanks and rascals. He had good friends, all knights of the same rank, and one of them was due to pay him back for the value of three horses. A deadline for payment was set and when the time came, Tundale went in search of his debtor, who gave him a sincere welcome. After a period of three days, Tundale asked him to settle his debt. "I do not have enough money," the other man answered, while appealing to his sense of goodwill: "Grant me a further delay! Come, let us go eat."

Tundale removed his armor, sat down, and began to eat, but was suddenly so touched by the power of God—who could no longer tolerate watching him lead such a sinful life—that he was unable to bring the hand reaching for the food on the table back to his mouth. With terrible howls he asked his companion's wife: "Protect my arms and armor, I am going to die!" and he immediately fell to the ground, stiff as death as if he had never lived, and he showed all the signs of having died because his soul had been carried away from him.[4]

The servants rushed in and stripped the table bare; the host and his guests began to weep. Tundale's body was turned over and back again in search of a sign of life: his sudden death astounded the doctors and distressed everyone there as well as all the residents of the town. There he was, lying prone as if dead on the tenth hour of Wednesday until the same time on Saturday. There was no thought given to burying him because there was a bit of warmth on the left side of his chest. At the aforementioned hour, the body recovered its soul and remained in the same condition save for a very faint breathing.

After an hour had passed, Tundale began breathing normally again. He was asked if he wished to take communion, and he nodded. After taking the sacred host, he praised and thanked God, and said: "O God, how great is Your mercy because of my misdeeds, of which there are many. O almighty God, how many immense torments You have shown me, but You protected me from them, restored to me my life, and I give thanks to You for Your infinite mercy!" Touched by divine grace, the knight gave away all he owned, took up the cross, and lived a life spent in holy devotion. He revealed to all who wished to listen to him what he had seen, heard, or suffered during those three days.

When my poor soul left my body, it was made aware of all its sins, which sent it into a state of immense and unspeakable torment. My soul was so scared it did not know what to do. It wanted to return to my body, but this was in vain, and it was so terrified that it could only set its hopes on divine mercy. It was then that something opened the eyes of my soul so it could see the approach of an unspeakable troop of gruesome devils.

There were so many of these devils that they filled the courtyard, the house, and all the small streets of the town. And while they were gathering around my soul, they were all speaking to me: "Poor soul, we are going to sing you the song of eternal death because you are fodder for the fires of hell, friend of darkness, and enemy of the eternal light!" They converged on my poor soul, biting it wickedly, and scratching its cheeks with their fingernails in rage,[5] and they went on to say: "Look, wretched soul, here are those you have served and with whom you will be going to hell because of your sins, the scope of which has never been equaled! You can be arrogant, but where now is your vanity and honor, why are you no longer acting so shamelessly, why are you hiding your hypocritical eyes? Where now is your strength, your proud speech, your lustful thoughts—has it all flown away?" These words sent my soul into the depths of terror. The devils tugged and plucked at my soul while trumpeting so all could hear: "You are in despair because you no longer have any hope in anyone. You are condemned to death eternal!" But merciful God does not truly desire the death of a sinner. He can offer consolation to all. By His Will, strength was given to my soul, and He helped it through its time of distress by sending it the help of an angel[6] that the soul saw shining in the distance like a star. When my soul caught sight of this glow, it gazed at it ardently and asked it to extricate it from its immense misery.

When the angel drew near to my soul it called me by name and said: "Greetings, Tundale!" I responded, full of joy and fear, with tears in my eyes: "O beloved lord, I wail to you about my distress because I am surrounded by horrible infernal punishments and shackled by the chains of eternal death!"

"Now you call me lord, but you never wished to acknowledge me when I accompanied you each day," replied the angel.

"O beloved lord, when would I have ever been able to see you? When was it ever possible for me to have heard your sweet voice?"

"I have followed you since birth,[7] and I have offered you the best advice, but you never endeavored to follow my counsel."

The angel then pointed at one devil standing among all the others.

"Look, there is the advisor you have always heeded and who is the reason you have forgotten God. However, His mercy is greater than His severity and He has taken pity on you. Rejoice, for you have been freed of the punishments that you deserve, and you shall only need to suffer a portion of them. Follow me and remember well all that you will see, and all that I am going to show you, because, once you have been returned to your fleshly body, they will be useful to you!"

This was when my soul, with a sense of great bitterness, separated from my body on which it had stood, and approached the angel. When the devils who surrounded me saw and realized that they were not able to torture and afflict me as they had hoped, and as had been promised to them, they began shouting, accusing God of being unjust.

"O dreadful God, Where is Your justice now? Where are Your words that state You wish people to pay by the worth of their actions? You are not keeping Your word because You are saving the person You wish to damn, and You damn the person You wish to save!"

After the lamentations of the devils ceased, they began punching and fighting each other, and leaving an indescribable stench behind them, they moved away from the angel.

"Lord, if you go first and I follow you, the horrible demons will grab me and cast me into eternal fire," I said.

The angel answered: "Have no fear, God has granted us His assistance. You should be aware that there are a thousand devils to your left and a thousand devils to your right, but not one of them will be capable of doing you any harm, and with your own eyes you shall see what reward God grants the sinner: eternal torment! You shall only suffer a portion of this and avoid the worst, thanks to Him."

I followed the angel and saw no other light but the one emanating from him for the entirety of our walk.

The Punishment of Killers and Murderers

We then made our way into a valley full of wailing and filled with furious flames and covered with incandescent fire, and the heat of the lid was much more violent than that of our fire. Countless souls were cast into this fire where they were melted like bits of grease thrown into a cooking pan. Once the souls had melted down, they were poured through the iron lid, which was seven ells in thickness, and then pressed through a sack as if they were wax. Once they had traveled through the cover into the fire, all the souls fell into new, indescribable torments.[8]

When I saw this great tribulation my poor soul went dark, and I spoke to the angel: "O beloved lord, if you are fully of a mind to, can you tell me what the souls who must endure this torment have done?"

The angel answered: "These torments are first and foremost intended for the killers, those who have killed their own mother and father, and for all those who, through their counsel or deeds, have contributed to their death. They then fall into an even greater torment as you shall soon see.

I then asked him: "Beloved angel, must I also suffer this brutal punishment?"

The angel replied: "You will not have to endure it although you have certainly earned it, for you, too, are a murderer. You must therefore pay penance and repent once you have been restored to your body, in order to avoid an even greater punishment."

The angel continued: "Follow me! We have a high mountain ahead of us." I followed the angel and we came to the foot of a steep mountain that was most alarming to behold. A narrow path crossed over it. On one side there was a fiery spring full of brimstone and pitch; the pit on the other side was ruled by an intense, extreme cold due to the wind, snow, and ice. Both sides of the mountain were filled with devils armed with three-pointed forks of burning fire that they used to jab the poor souls in torment. On one side of the mountain there were souls burning in brimstone and pitch. Then, with the help of their pitchforks, the devils cast them into the pit on the other side, into the intense, freezing cold, then back from the cold into the furnace. When I saw this strange punishment and realized that I would have to follow this narrow path to cross over this horrible mountain, I said to the angel: "O beloved lord, how can my poor soul cross over on this path when I can see on either side my eternal damnation?"

The angel responded: "Have no fear." And I followed him.

The Punishment of Those Who Died of Pride

Once we had crossed over the mountain, we came to a deep valley whose bottom was beyond my sight. I could hear the distressing clamor of souls burning in heat and smoke coming out of the very entrails of the mountain.[9] Above this cruel valley, going from one mountain to the next, there was a footbridge[10] that was one thousand steps in length and one foot wide. No one who had not been chosen by God would have been able to cross it. Countless souls were falling from this footbridge into the valley, and I could see a terrified priest advancing on it. He was well dressed and carried a palm frond in his hand.

When I caught sight of the narrow footbridge and the immense suffering that took place beneath it, I asked the angel: "O beloved lord, if only it was your will that I not have to cross this narrow bridge!"

He looked at me kindly and said: "You will be spared the ordeal of

this footbridge, but you will have to take another that is much more terrifying." This was how I was able to reach the other side of this footbridge without suffering any harm, thanks to the clemency of this angel. I was overcome with happiness and I said to him: "Beloved lord, if it is clearly your wish, tell me what souls dwell in this valley of suffering."

The angel responded: "In this valley, tormented for eternity, are all those who died in pride or who, through their counsel or actions, helped others who suffer the same fate. But in the mountain you see before us, are tortured all those who have not been able to live in accordance with truth and who have resisted their superiors."

Here Now Follows the Punishment of Usurers, Brigands, Thieves, and Misers

When we came to the edge of the mountain, I saw a large, terrifying animal, which was more fear-inspiring and larger than the mountain we had seen earlier. Its eyes looked like deep pits, and its maw gaped so wide that nine thousand armored men could have entered it. Two immense, fully armored giants[11] were standing inside its throat. One of them had its head turned toward the beast's upper teeth; the other giant had its feet pointed at its upper teeth and its head toward its lower teeth.

They were planted in the animal's mouth like two columns dividing it into three gates out from which poured flames escaping from a

terrible inferno. A large number of devils were standing in front of this beast where they were pushing and chasing many souls toward these three doors and into this frightful beast's very throat. I could hear the most terrifying array of howls coming from the depths of this beast, along with the screams and tears of thousands of men and women.

After we contemplated the animal for a long time and listened to the distressing cries of the souls it had swallowed, I turned to the angel with tears in my eyes and gripped by fear, and said: "O beloved lord, do you not see this terrifying, enormous beast before us? How can you draw so close to it?"

"It is here where our path should lead us, for only the chosen few can avoid this punishment. The name of this beast is Achernus Achyro,[12] and it not only devours those who enrich themselves through the practice of usury, robbery, and theft, and those who were jealous, lied, played around, and were the servants of lust, and devoted themselves to worldly living, but it also swallows those who desired and acquired ill-gotten gains and possessed more than they needed. The two giants that are imprisoned in the animal's mouth are named Justus and Connaulus.[13] All these torments you have just witnessed are immense, but you shall see many others that are even greater, and you will not be spared some of the suffering they cause."

He drew closer to the beast, and I was compelled to follow him, more and more terrified, and as I was in the midst of all this suffering, he vanished and I found myself alone.

Once the devils—there were over one hundred thousand—realized that the angel had left, they came running with the speed of rabid dogs and dragged me into the animal's mouth. Once I was inside it, my soul suffered indescribable pains caused by the beasts that were already there: bears, lions, wolves, dogs, and demons. And if I do not describe these sufferings in greater detail, know that of my life on earth, these were the most intense torments I have ever suffered, but they were well deserved because my sins were a daily provocation to divine wrath.

I rent my cheeks doubting that any help would be forthcoming, but I found myself released from these torments without knowing how. As I lay there in my weakened state, I opened my eyes and saw the angel shining in the distance.

In great relief I exclaimed: "O hope and divine consolation! O my light and savior, how could you leave me in this immense distress? Poor wretch that I am, how may I thank God for His goodness? Even if his sole grace was only to entrust me to you, how am I to thank Him?"

"Give a thought to what you just said! His goodness is greater than all your misdeeds, and He judges everyone in accordance with their actions. When you are restored to your body, try to remember the suffering you have endured because of your crimes and sin no more!"

The Punishment for Those Who Rob the Poor and Steal Church Property

"Now let us continue forward! You are going to soon see even greater torments." But I was unable to walk because of the many tortures I had suffered. The angel touched me, I was healed, and I followed him until we arrived to a reeking swamp whose entire surface was on fire. The smoke was so thick and the flames so fierce that it was impossible to see the sky. A huge number of animals could be seen here tormenting and imprisoning the souls in their care. In order to cross this bottomless marsh there was a footbridge that was two miles long and two spans wide. It was studded with pointed nails that were placed closely together, and the person forced to take this bridge was obliged to place their feet on their sharp points. The beasts beneath the footbridge had extremely long necks that were quite fat and looked like towers that spit out fire. This was the reason the swamp stank so badly and was burning so fiercely. I saw a soul on this same bridge who was screaming, weeping, and cursing; it was carrying a huge burden of wheat on its back and was compelled to carry it although the sharpened nails caused it dreadful pain. But the soul did not truly feel it because of its dread of the terrifying beasts that sought to pull it down into this terrible swamp.

The sight of this harsh punishment filled me with terror, and I turned to the angel and said: "O beloved lord, if it is your will, I would truly like to know why the soul must carry this heavy load of wheat while crossing this abominable footbridge."

The angel replied to me: "Normally, this punishment would be your fate as it is to all those who have committed the same sins as you, those who have stolen. Whether the theft is a trifle or extremely large, it matters not, you are still a thief, and it is necessary to punish minor sins and great ones alike. Different and unique punishments are inflicted upon those who commit the sin called 'sacrilege.'"

And he added: "He who steals a sacred object or even one that is not yet in a holy place,[14] the religious servants who have the appearance and garb of saints but who do not fulfill their duties, are those whose souls shall not return to God because they have made a false holiness. All these souls must cross through the ordeal of this footbridge if they do not repent and perform penance. An even greater punishment then awaits them. Prepare yourself as we are not going to travel through it! You are probably able to cross it by the grace of divine power, but it will not permit me to carry you to the other side. I will not go over there without you. You will have to cross through it without my help, but you will not be alone as you must bring a wild cow with you, safe and sound, to the other side."

My soul began weeping bitterly and answered: "Woe is me! O why did God create me knowing that he would cause me to suffer such atrocious torment? How will I be able to lead a wild cow to the other side when I cannot even set foot on this narrow footbridge! May divine mercy come to my aid!"

"Remember how when you were still alive you stole a cow from your cohort."

"O beloved angel, you are fully aware that I returned it to him."

"Yes, because you cannot remove it from my gaze, which is why you will not have to suffer the full torment of this punishment because an evil intention alone is a lesser sin compared to its realization, although both are reprehensible. You remain frozen there; can't you see the cow?"

I moaned about my sins, took hold of the animal, and made my way forth to the footbridge. Horrific beasts in the swamp immediately sprang to attention in hope I would fall in so they could devour me. My first steps were pathetic; the cow did not wish to follow me. When I stumbled, it pushed ahead. When I stepped forward it halted; when I clung to it, we both fell down, then got back up as one, and things proceeded this way until we reached the middle of the footbridge. We encountered a soul carrying a huge load of wheat on its back there and were unable to cross past it. This was not the same as mercy meeting truth, or justice meeting peace.[15]

The soul asked for me to let it pass, but neither of us could take a step forward or back. We were stuck there, and our suffering was great because the nails pierced our feet and their blood turned the footbridge red. While we both expressed remorse for our sins, we passed before each other, I don't know how. The angel, whom I had left behind me, now spoke to me amicably: "Welcome! Worry no more about the cow; you have been freed of it." I showed him my injured feet while saying: "I am incapable of going further."

"Soul, you were quick to sin and cause blood to flow; this is why it would be just to force you to march eternally over dire, bloodstained paths if divine mercy did not offer you its aid."

He then healed me and commanded me to follow him.

What Follows Tells of the Punishment of Those Who Are Religious Ecclesiastics— Priests, Monks and Nuns—in Appearance

"Beloved angel, where are we going now?" I asked.

"A terrible torturer named Pristinus awaits us. We are not able to avoid him and we must enter his home. His house is ever full of guests, but he always requires more that he will be able to torture."

We continued on our way that now led us into a wild and shadow-haunted mountain until we arrived before a large gaping gate, from which spilled a light similar to that of an oven. Fierce flames leaped from this door and burned all the souls who found themselves within a thousand feet of its proximity.

When I caught sight of this spectacle, I refused to approach any closer as I had already been burned before. I told the angel: "What should I do now? I am headed toward the gates of eternal death! Who will help me now?"

"You shall be saved from this fire and its flames; however, you must enter them."

As I drew closer to the angel, I could see many butchers with axes, hatchets, knives, and other kinds of tools they were using to dismember and cut up the souls that were standing in the midst of flames that were hotter than fire. My distress doubled, and I told the angel: "Please

spare me from this torment and I will agree to undergo those that we are going to see later."

"This punishment is greater than all those you have seen thus far, but you have yet to see another one that far exceeds the imagination. Don't you see the devils are like rabid dogs and are waiting for you to enter?"

I begged the angel to spare me this torment, but he refused. When the devils saw that I heeded his wishes and was now in their power, they raced to meet me, beating me and then cutting me into tiny pieces that they cast into the burning house. No one could imagine the pain and suffering that reigned there, wails, gnashing of teeth, hunger and thirst. Here they were tortured in the limbs and hidden parts of the body that had been used by men and women in the service of pleasure and immodesty. It seemed to me that these limbs were not only those of lay people but included the body parts of priests, monks, and nuns, and all of them were covered by vile worms. The higher their position during their lifetime, the greater their suffering. On seeing these souls tortured like I had been, I acknowledged my sins, which would have rightfully earned me this punishment, but divine will spared me from it, I don't know how. [. . .]

Here Is the Punishment of Lustful Priests, Monks, and Nuns

"We should leave here without delay," the angel now said, "for we have other punishments to see. Once we have finished with these ordeals, we can then take a look at the joys offered by heaven."

We came to a place where I saw a horrible beast that had two wings, a very long neck, a large beak, and iron claws. Fierce flames were springing forth from its mouth—flames that no one could extinguish. This animal moved about over a frozen marsh and swallowed every soul it was able to grab. Once the souls in torment had vanished inside the beast's belly, it spit them back out into the marsh. There they were then made ready for new torments. All the souls, those of both men and women, that had traveled through the beast's belly before entering the

marsh, had been gifted with the body of an animal—a snake or viper.[16] Like a pregnant woman, these souls had to wait for the time fixed for them to be born carrying these heavy burdens.

While waiting for this moment to come, they were bitten on the inside by the fangs of the viper and tortured on the outside by the intense cold of the marsh. When the time arrived for these tormented souls—both men and women—to deliver themselves of this shameful fruit, they proceeded to fill the depths of hell with the echo of their wretched cries. This birth did not only take place by the hips, in conformance with the nature of reptiles and serpents, but also by the arms, legs, heart, eyes, mouth, ears, ribs, and all the other parts of the body. What they gave birth to was nothing but vipers and serpents with burning heads and sharp beaks that they used to shred the bodies of their poor hosts as they tried to come out. But their curved hooks prevented them from emerging.[17] The reptiles then bit the souls with their poisonous iron beaks until their veins and limbs began to fall into pieces. Of all the cries to be heard there, the most violent ones were those coming from the vipers and the souls who were enduring this punishment. If the devils had known any mercy, they would have taken pity on these sufferers, because all sorts of vile animals were climbing over the limbs of the souls. They were suffering terribly from being tortured this way.

At the sight of this terrifying punishment I asked the angel: "I beg you tell me, beloved lord, what sins these poor souls might have committed to have to endure such an ordeal?"

"I told you earlier that the members of the religious orders whose knowledge and good works honor God, as well as the men of the clergy and lay people who devote their lives to Him, out of fear and out of gratitude for His clemency, will all find an even greater bliss in the Kingdom of Heaven. But those who break the rules of morality and live without respecting God while they have received countless gifts from His hands, and those who have not used them in His honor, and all those who forgot to repent while still on earth, their torments will be even greater than those inflicted on those people who received only a small portion of divine gifts. The priests, nuns, canons, monks, men of the clergy, and all those who wear sacred habits, who never think to thank God for His very great mercy, and lead a sinful life by indulging in lust, pride, and other sins, will all suffer this punishment: the very parts of their bodies will be torn asunder by vipers and snakes. Soul, be aware that this torment is destined for all those leading a lustful life on this world be they men or women, members of the clergy or lay people." [. . .]

It was at this point that Tundale's soul came to the bath of eternal death.

We came to a path that led to a high mountain, but the more I walked toward it the further away it became and the more my hopes of ever climbing it shrank.

"Where does this path lead," I asked the angel.

"It leads to hell and to eternal death," the angel replied.

"Since this path is so narrow and so hard, and we cannot see anyone that is using it, why do the Scriptures tell us it is wide and that many men follow it?" I asked.

"They are not speaking about this path; the one they mean is a life of sin like greed, lasciviousness, wrath, hatred, and intemperance. Those who dedicate their lives to it are taking the path of eternal death unless they make atonement. Follow me!"

A long and gloomy road led us into a valley echoing with mournful cries and lamentations. I could see forges there and much iron: this is where the terrible clamor of souls and demons was coming from.

"O beloved lord, can you hear that?" I asked the angel.

"Yes!"

"What do you call this torment?"

"A smith named Vulcanus lives here. He draws many souls into his home and tortures them thousands upon thousands of times."

"Tell me, must I, too, experience this punishment?"

The angel nodded and I followed him sorrowfully. The smiths came racing toward me and grabbed me with their burning hot tongs that they used to toss me into the inferno at the top of the oven, in which there were already some one hundred thousand souls. They stoked the flames with their bellows and we, the souls inside this blaze, melted into it. Then with their tongs they would pluck out some ten, twenty, thirty, or even one hundred souls, place them on their anvil, and beat them for such a long time with their hammers that they formed one single block. The souls could not die and begged God to kill them, and called for death to deliver them, but it fled their pleas. After the devils had beaten the souls for a sufficiently long time, they asked if they had been forged well enough. The other devils and hammerers yelled: "Toss them to us and we will tell you!" The smiths then cast them to the others, who caught them on their pitchforks of white-hot iron, then beat them with

their own hammers even harder than the previous smiths, until the souls were practically annihilated. My angel came in and pulled me free of this place and said: "Do you not regret having led the life of pride, licentiousness, and pleasure that has caused your current suffering?"

My weakened and powerless soul could only sigh piteously, whereupon he offered me consolation: "Be reassured! God alone leads souls into hell and He is the only one that can lead them out. All of those you have seen are waiting for the Last Judgment. But you have not yet reached the true hell, come!"

We came to a place that was home to an intense cold and intolerable stench. In terror, I asked the angel: "Just what is this place? The earth is shaking! I dare not move, I'm scared!" But he vanished, and I was in despair to find myself in a situation with no assistance or consolation. I could hear the souls screaming, weeping, and crying, followed by a huge clap of thunder. I then noticed that these noises were coming from a pit that was square like a cistern. A pestilential smoke was pouring out of it, and there were flames in its center in which more than one hundred thousand demons were standing with an equal number of souls who were flying through the clouds like sparks, before falling back into the pit, which was similar to a blazing oven. I wished to retreat but was paralyzed where I stood and began lamenting my fate. When the devils heard me, they came running with their claws extended and surrounded me, saying: "You have earned eternal punishment; here we find you in tears, you have learned what suffering and affliction truly are, but you must undergo even greater torment before you come to the well of life. Walk forward and no longer put your hope in anyone! You will never again see the light and no one shall come to your aid. Know that you have come to the gates of hell, which you must enter, for you have been deceived by the one who brought you here."

Then the devils huddled together asking: "Why do you remain frozen there? Why are we waiting to carry this soul into the abyss and hand it over to Lucifer, our master?"

But the angel then appeared and drove them away.

HOW TUNDALE'S SOUL CAME TO THE GATES OF HELL AND SAW LUCIFER IN CHAINS

"Come and see, I am going to show you the enemy of all!" The angel crossed through the doors of hell and went on to say: "Look! Those who dwell here are denied light for all eternity and they are unable to see us." I advanced and looked into the depths of hell. Even if I had one thousand heads, each of which possessed one thousand tongues, I would not be able to describe even the least of the punishments I saw there. I caught sight of Lucifer, the prince of hell; his size was far greater than that of any of the animals I had seen before. He had a thousand hands, each of which was one hundred ells in length and was ten ells in thickness. The same was true about his feet. He had an enormous mouth and his tail, which was as long as that of a dragon, was sharpened to abuse the lost souls.

He was bound to an iron grill, upon which numerous devils armed with bellows were fanning the flames in the embers, and surrounded by countless souls. Lucifer was being roasted. In a rage he threw himself to one side and then the other, causing the whole of hell to shake.

He grabbed every soul within reach, then tore them into pieces, and crushed them into dust. Next, with his burning breath, he would send them flying all around him. Once he had finished exhaling his nauseating breath, he would suck in all the souls he had breathed out. Those who tried to flee him he would stab with his tail, but he would also stab himself. He was thus both tortured victim and torturer.

"Tell me his name?" I asked the angel.

"His name is Lucifer, he was the first creature created by God. He was called Light Bearer of all the angels because of his greatness, and he dwelled in heaven. If he were ever able to escape hell, he would darken the sky and the earth, even into its very depths. The vast crowd surrounding him consists of demons and souls from the time of Adam—all of them are damned and cursed. [. . .] Now," said the angel, "it is time to follow another path to come to our kingdom.

I then saw a very high wall, beneath which countless souls were suffering from the intense cold caused by rain and a bitter wind. They were also beaten down with hunger and thirst. Despite all this suffering, they were bathed in light, and no pestilence could be smelled coming from them.

"Who are they that are living here?" I asked the angel.

"These are the souls of those who behaved egotistically and never gave out alms."

Continuing our journey, we came to a gate that opened by itself and offered entry into a magnificent world overflowing with flowers and delectable odors. The number of souls in jubilation was beyond count. Here night never fell and the sun never set, and a well with the water of life was also here. I forgot all my suffering because bliss and happiness reigned supreme here.

I asked my angel: "Tell me, who are the souls that come here, and what is the name of this well?"

"Here is where the good people come to dwell; although they are spared all torment, they are not worthy of the joys that are offered by the well of the water of life.[18] Whoever drinks it but once will never again have thirst and live eternally."

I then caught sight of some people I knew and was surprised to see two kings in their midst, Contaber* and Donat.† "Both of these individuals were powerful men, hard on earth and mortal enemies. How were they able to be reconciled, and how did they become deserving of this happiness?"

"Contaber was ill for a long time," the angel answered. "He praised God and wished to become a monk. Captured and held as a prisoner for a long time, Donat offered all his worldly goods for the love of God."

A short while later we came to a house with richly decorated walls, a silver roof, and precious stones. It had no doors or windows, but anyone who wanted was able to go inside. The interior glowed with light as if many suns were shining from inside. It was long and wide, and the entire floor was made of gold with precious gems. I saw a golden chair that was fitted out with silk and richly decorated. A king named Tormax‡ was seated upon this throne; he had been my lord on earth. I remained there in a state of complete amazement while radiant figures brought him presents and praised him. Clergymen came in wearing

*That is to say, Conchobar Ua Briain, king of Munster from 1127 to 1142.

†Donnchadh Mac Carthaigh, king of Thomond from 1127 to 1142; died in 1144.

‡Cormac Mac Carthaigh, king of Desmond from 1124 to 1138, and brother of Donnchadh Mac Carthaigh.

their liturgical robes, richly embroidered in gold and precious stones that were so brilliant they sparkled, and this was enough to procure eternal joy. They set chalices, monstrances, and jewels before Tormax, then knelt before him saying: "You are blessed and will be fed with the fruits of your labor."[19]

I turned toward the angel: "I am wondering where this king, who was my lord on earth, has found so many servants, as I do not recognize a single one of them."

"These are not the ones that served him on earth, but the poor to whom he gave alms. For this he is receiving his eternal reward."

"I would truly like to know if this king was punished for his sins after he died."

"He was indeed punished for them and still suffers every day, as you will see in a moment."

The light grew darker, Tormax stood up in tears, left the house, and fire began to burn him. The flames reached as high as his navel, and he was wearing a hair shirt over the top of his body.

"He suffers like this for three hours a day," the angel told me. "Then he rests for twenty-one hours."

"Why does he endure this pain?"

"He defiled his conjugal life, this is why the fire only burns him up to his navel. He is wearing a hair shirt over the top of his body because

he had a count slain evilly. His other sins have been forgiven, but not these. Come, let us keep going."

We came to a very high, handsome wall made entirely of silver. It seemed to have no door, and I don't know how I was able to get through it.

Once I had entered, I saw the choir of saints and angels, men and women dressed in white, singing praises to God. [. . .] Their voices were wonderfully sweet, echoing like the melodies of stringed instruments, and they gave off an aroma of holiness more delectable than that of the most exquisite herbs. I wanted to stay here, but the angel retorted: "There is even a more beautiful reward, the one given to the good and faithful couples who offered good guidance to their servants and shared their goods with the poor, the pilgrims, and the churches. [. . .] We shall need to climb even higher to gaze upon the kingdom of the blessed."

We went forward and came across souls who were jubilant. They greeted us and praised God for having saved me.

A little further on, a new wall[20] loomed before us, which was as high as the one before it, but made entirely of pure gold. We then saw golden chairs and thrones that were adorned with precious stones and covered with different kinds of silk. Men and women were there, their faces as radiant as the sun at its zenith. All were wearing golden crowns decorated with gemstones, and they were seated behind lecterns that

were holding books written in gold script while singing hallelujah. "These are the people who abjured their bodies, those who performed the duties of God, and who suffered martyrdom in Christ's name," the angel told me when I asked.

Here Be Other Joys and Honors

As Tundale's soul gazed at the surrounding area, it spied a castle and tents of purple, silver, and gold, from which emerged the sound of organs, harps, and many stringed instruments.

"What kind of souls are listening to this music?" I asked the angel.

"They are the souls of monks and nuns who conducted themselves

with piety, did penance, and gladly obeyed their superiors. [. . .] They are tasting the delights of heaven; [. . .] they have earned these times in which they never stop singing the praises of their Redeemer and the Bestower of all good."

"I would like to join them, to see and hear them."

"I would dearly love for you to see and hear them, but you should not enter their tents because they are performing in the presence of the Holy Trinity. Whoever enters forgets the world of mortals. Only a virgin deserves the honor of joining the choir of holy angels."

We drew nearer to these tents and saw many souls that looked like angels, and whose radiance, beautiful fragrance, and voice far outstripped in sweetness and gaiety any melody played on a string instrument. Not a hand or a lip could be seen to move; the sound resonated by means of the will of each individual. Chains of pure gold were hanging above their heads on which cymbals, small bells, and lilies, also made of gold, were attached. In the midst of all this, groups of angels soared about on their golden wings singing.

Here Is the Fate That Awaits All Those Who Have Built Churches, Those That Protected Them, and Those That Took Part by Means of Their Counsel or Actions

I felt such intense pleasure that my soul wished only to remain there, but the angel told me: "Look!" I then saw a large, grand tree covered by all manner of leaves, fruits, and flowers. Multicolored birds were gathered on its branches to sing. Beneath its branches a myriad of lilies, roses, and delicate herbs were bursting from the ground and giving off an exquisite aroma. In the shelter of the tree a large number of gold and ivory cells could be seen in which many people were praising and blessing God for His beneficence and His gifts. Each of these individuals, who were dressed as monks, wore a gold crown and carried a scepter.

"What is this tree?" I asked.

"It is the symbol of the Church," the angel answered. "The people you see gathered beneath it are those who placed all their zeal in building and protecting it."

Continuing on our way, we came to the foot of another wall, one that was taller and even more beautiful than those I had seen before. It was made of precious stones of all colors—crystals, chrysolites, jaspers, amethysts, emeralds, sapphires, onyxes, topazes, garnets, and sard stones.* [. . .] We climbed over the wall and experienced, heard, and felt something that most likely no one had ever experienced, heard, or felt:

*They are the stones of the heavenly Jerusalem (see Revelation 21:19–20).

the nine choirs of angels. I heard inexpressible words that it would be wrong to speak aloud and that no one is capable of defining. [. . .]

"Daughter," the angel told my soul, "listen and forget all else!" [. . .]

Saint Ruadan, My Patron in the Land of Hibernia

My soul was there when Saint Ruadan,* a confessor, embraced it with great joy and told my soul: "May God protect you from the beginning, from the return, and for all time![21] I am Saint Ruadan, the one who can grant your desire." He then vanished.

Here I Saw Four Bishops I Knew Well

Looking around me, I caught sight of the apostle Patrick in the company of numerous bishops, among whom were four that I knew well: the archbishop Celestin;† Malachias‡ who had come from Rome during the time of Innocent; his brother Christian,§ the bishop of Lyon; and Nemias,¶ famous for his wisdom and chastity. One throne was unoccupied and I asked: "Why is it empty, and who is it intended for?"

"It belongs to one of our brothers who is still living, and he shall take his seat upon it when he dies," Malachias told me.

Then the angel asked me: "Have you fully contemplated all this bliss?"

"Yes," my soul answered. "And I pray for you to leave me here for eternity."

"No, you must return to your body and reveal to Christians all you have seen and heard."

"O beloved lord, why must I leave these delights?"

"You cannot remain here because you did not remain chaste, and

*Ruadhán Mac Fergusa Birn (died 584), one of the apostles of Ireland.

†Celestinus Arthmachanus (Ceallach Mac Aedha; Saint Celsus), bishop of Armagh and Coarb (1105–1129).

‡Máel Maedóc (Saint Malachy), archbishop of Armagh (1127–1137).

§Gilla Críst Ua Morgair (Saint Christian), bishop of Clogher and of Lough (died 1138).

¶Gilla-na-naemh Ua Muircheartaigh, bishop of Cloyne (1140–1149).

you sought not to believe in the Holy Scriptures. Return to your body, refrain from sinning, be virtuous, and my aid and counsel shall never be refused to you because I will remain faithfully by your side."

As soon as the angel spoke these words, I returned to where I was lying. And when I started to move, I felt a weight that was nothing other than the heavy burden of my body. This all took place in the blink of an eye. And when I feebly opened my eyes, I saw the priests who had been keeping watch over me for three days. I took communion

and gave all my worldly goods to the poor,[22] drew the Holy Cross on my clothing, and revealed everything that I had seen and heard. [. . .]

May any who finds it impossible to believe this story know that it is never too late to repent and that punishment for our sins awaits us here or in the Otherworld. This is where the book of Tundale ends.

Tondolus der Ritter (Speyer: Hist, ca. 1495)

📖 Text: Palmer, ed. *Tondolus der Ritter.*

📖📖 Micha, *Voyages dans l'au-delà*; Palmer, *"Visio Tnugdali"*; Wagner, ed. *Visio Tnugdali lateinisch und altdeutsch.*

3. GUESTS OF THE DEVIL (LATIN)

The following story shows us how it is possible to cross over into the Otherworld without realizing it. Thanks to some revealing clues, the traveler eventually discovers where he is. To the best of our knowledge, there is no other text like this one in medieval literature.

A large number of minstrels flooded to the wedding of a powerful Saxon lord, as was customary. Among them was a minstrel of great renown whose name was Vollarc. Like all famous men, he did not travel alone but with other minstrels in a procession similar to that of knights. One day as they were riding along, they were joined by a devil on horseback who had assumed the guise of a worthy gentleman, and they engaged in friendly conversation. While they were getting along so famously, they asked the newcomer his name. "I am called Nithard," the disguised devil answered—a word that translated into Latin means "odious" or "very evil," and he had been given this name as the source of all evil and hatred in the world. But neither Vollarc nor any of his companions suspected his true identity. As evening began to fall, they began deliberating about where they should sleep for the night, and the devil told them: "If you would come with me, I will give you lodging. My home is close by. However, I have the worst possible valets and vassals. You should avoid going near them or speaking to them." Everyone accepted his offer.

Like a guide, he assumed a position at the front of the party, and they proceeded to enter a long valley, followed by a dark forest. They were then met by torchbearers, many of whom were richly clad, who took great care of their horses, then showed them into the lordly dwelling with walls that were covered with precious fabrics. A table was then set on which the minstrels could see dishes of silver and gold. Vollarc and his companions felt great admiration for the premises and, mindful of their host's warning, did not speak to anyone. They thought this invitation was a manifestation of divine grace, whereas in reality it was pure deviltry. They went out to see their horses and were delighted to find them so well fed.

When the time for dinner came, numerous servants appeared, bearing a wealth of food and drink served on magnificent plates and in magnificent goblets. They all thought they must be in the home of a rich king. Cheered by the meal and wine, Vollarc grew emboldened and, in the way of performers, which is to say brazenly, he questioned his host: "Lord, permit me to ask you a question! I am very curious as to where such a profusion of gold and silver, and so much food and drink, and all this wealth that I see around you, the likes of which I have never seem at the home of any prince, has come from." The devil answered: "You should not be surprised because all these goods are those that the churches and monasteries have unjustly stolen from widows and the poor. They were all acquired criminally and all came back to me!" Vollarc remained dumbstruck and, curbing his anguish, smiled so that the devil would suspect nothing of his terror, and invoked God to enter his heart.

Once the meal was over and all were sitting here and there, Vollarc left and gathered his companions. "Woe is us," he said. "We have stumbled into the lair of perdition! The prince that gave us welcome and shown us all his pomp and prowess is the devil—that is certain. I therefore ask you to put yourselves in the hands of God and to beg him with all your strength that he show us signs of His mercy and allow us to escape. But we must remain circumspect in every way! Now, let us go back and act as if nothing has happened."

They rejoined their host, and when they were asked if they wanted more wine, they acquiesced. After pretending to drink, Vollarc asked the devil if he would allow them to take their leave. "Tomorrow," the devil responded. "Today we shall amuse ourselves together. It is also necessary that the gifts I intend to give you are brought here so you can leave tomorrow without delay." Shivering inside, the minstrel assented.

That evening, the devil gave them their presents: gold and silver vessels, as well as luxurious clothing that he distributed to each minstrel before granting them permission to leave. While doing this, he told them: "Here is everything I promised you. Tomorrow I will lead you back to your route." He then addressed his valets, adding: "Tomorrow, at the appointed hour, accompany our guests back to where they will know where they are!" That said, Vollarc and his companions went to their rooms, replete. Studying the valuable gifts of the devil they were

unable to find sleep and prayed to God all night long, "crying toward him in their distress and He delivered them from their anguish."[23]

In the morning their guides set them back upon the right path asking: "Is this truly the path by which you came?" The minstrels replied: "We know where to go from here!" Their guides then vanished quite suddenly.

Once Vollarc and his companions found themselves alone, they felt weak from hunger as well as their horses, who were barely able to drag themselves forward, and when they looked at the presents they had received, all they found were spiderwebs.[24] This gave proof of what God said about the devil in the Gospels: "There is no truth in him. When he speaks his lies, he pulls them from his own depths because he is a liar and the father of lies."[25]

OTLOH OF ST. EMMERAN, *LIBER VISIONUM,* CHAPTER 23

This story, which was recorded by Saint Otloh of St. Emmeran (ca. 1010–1067), makes use of the diabolical illusion whereby food and gifts reveal deception. This detail can be found in numerous tales in which fantasy beings offer wealth to the heroes, but the treasures always turn out to be coal or leaves.

Otloh von St. Emmeram, *Liber Visionum.*

three

Travels in the Land of Faery

1. THOMAS OF ERCELDOUNE (MODERN SCOTS)

Thomas of Erceldoune, nicknamed Thomas the Rhymer, was a Scottish poet and seer of the thirteenth century. Legend maintains that he stayed for some time at the home of the Queen of the Fairies, or Elves, and brought gifts back from his sojourn that were the source of his fame. This legend enjoyed considerable popularity in the nineteenth century, and great writers like Theodor Fontane in Germany were inspired by it. Washington Irving borrowed from it to write his Rip Van Winkle *(1819).* Note: Line numbers and direct quotations are from the texts reproduced in *The Romance and Prophecies of Thomas of Erceldoune* (ed. Murray).

One beautiful May morning, Thomas of Erceldoune was singing as he made his way to Huntley Banks when he heard the song of blackbirds and larks echoing throughout the glade. While lost in his thoughts, as he lay beneath a tree, he spied a beautiful woman who came riding down the gentle slope of a hill.* Even if I should live until the day of the Last Judgment I could never describe the splendor of her beauty.

*This is a fairy mound (*síd, síth*), an entrance into the Celtic Otherworld.

The lady was seated upon a white palfrey; its saddle was encrusted with toadstones, diamonds, and pearls, and she herself shone like the mid-summer sun. The locks of her hair were floating in the wind, and she wore a gold horn around her neck. Sometimes she sang and sometimes she sounded her horn as she was riding across the meadows. Her garment was of green silk, over which she wore a velvet coat. Her stirrups were made of pure crystal, her reins of pure gold, and the small bells attached around the neck of her steed were tinkling. She was holding three dogs on a leash and carried several arrows stuck in her belt.

Thomas, beneath his tree, became lost in contemplation: "She must be the queen of heaven; she who bore the Child who died for us! If I should fail to speak with her, my heart will break of languor. I shall gather all my courage and attempt to meet her at the Eildon Tree."* He swiftly arose and traveled down the hill until he came to the Eildon Tree. There, beneath its green branches, he threw himself at the feet of the lady.

"Gracious queen of heaven, take pity on me!"

"Thomas, do not speak thus! I am not the queen of heaven; I have never risen so high. I am the queen of the fairies,[1] and even though I wear splendid garments I am merely hunting and my dogs are coming to my call."

"Fair lady, if you are here solely for pleasure, grant me the favor of letting me lie with you."[2]

"Thomas, that would be sheer madness! I beg you to leave me in peace at once because, and I am telling you true, that would ruin my beauty."

"Kind lady, take pity on me! I would like to live close by your side forever, whether you are in hell or in the torments of hell, I give you my word!"

"O mortal man,† this shall make me ugly, but let your will be done. Know that you are making the worst decision because my beauty shall be ruined because of it."

---

*A solitary tree that stood on the hills of Eildon, near Melrose.

†*Mane of molde,* the text reads (l. 117), "man of clay," which refers to man's creation by God.

The beautiful woman lay down upon the grass beneath the greenleaf where Thomas joined her. "This play pleases you," she told Thomas, "but you are going to disfigure my features for the entire day, so, please, I beg you, leave me be."

Thomas stood up and looked at the woman: her hair hung down in disarray about her face, the blue of her laughing eyes had become tarnished, her dress was torn, and her body was the color of melted lead.

"Alas and woe," he cried. "How horrible your face has become!" Her radiant face had become pale and faded.

"Say farewell, Thomas, to the sun, the moon, and the trees. For the time of twelve moons you must follow me and no longer see the world."*

He collapsed to his knees and said: "Take pity on me, merciful queen! Alas, what suffering! I must now pay for my sins. Jesus, I place my soul into your hands whatever becomes of my body." She led him to the foot of the Eildon Tree and into the secret place within the hill,[3] where it was dark as any midnight.[4] They waded through water[5] up to their knees, crossing through blood red waves because all the blood that flows on earth shall blend into the streams of this land.[6] For three days, Thomas heard naught but the murmur of the river until he burst out: "Oh woe is me! Hunger shall be my undoing."

The lady led him into a beautiful orchard where fruits grew in vast number. Pears, apples, and plums were ripening here, and the nightingale had built its nest in the branches of a fig tree. Parrots were flying here and there and the thrush was singing tirelessly. Tortured by hunger, Thomas stretched out his hand to take a fruit. "Stop!" the lady shouted, "for these fruits contain all the wounds of hell. I tell you, in all truthfulness, if you pick them your soul will be cast into the infernal flames.[7] Thomas, do what I tell you; lay your head in my lap and you will see the most beautiful vision—one no man on earth has ever seen."

---

*The poet uses the term *Middylle erthe,* "middle earth," here (l. 160), which corresponds to the name of the human world in Germanic cosmogony (Old English *middangeard,* Old Norse Miðgarðr, etc.).

He obeyed and she asked him: "Do you see that fair path that crosses through the high mountain? It is the road taken by the souls of the sinners once they have found redemption.* Now, do you see that other path below it that crosses through the greenery? That is the one that leads to the joys of paradise. And do you see the third path that crosses over the green plain? That is the one where the souls of sinners suffer. And do you see the fourth path at the bottom of this deep valley? It is the one on which the howls from the infernal furnace emerge. And finally, do you see that splendid castle on the high hill? There is none other like it on earth. It belongs to me as well as to the lord of this land. I would rather be hung or drowned than for him to learn that we lay together. When you are at this castle, I beg you to hold your tongue;[8] whatever you see or hear, answer only to me.† When my lord is at the table served by thirty-three proud knights, and I am in the seat of honor, I will tell him of our meeting at the Eildon Tree."

Stupefied, Thomas stared at the lordly lady who shone like ivory and rode her white palfrey as beautiful and finely adorned as before. Her hounds preceded her and she sounded her horn. Both took the path to the castle and entered the great hall. Many beautiful women approached and bowed before the sovereign while harps and fiddles could be heard playing, as well as minstrels. The knights danced three by three and all was revelry, games, and play, and women of marvelous beauty danced and sang. Fifty stags were carried in; dogs lapped up their blood while the cooks cut up the game with hunting knives.

Thomas dwelled there in the midst of pleasure I could not even begin to describe, until the day when the charming lady said to him: "Prepare to leave, for you cannot stay here any longer. Do it quickly, I shall accompany you to the Eildon Tree! He sadly replied: "Kind lady, permit me to stay here longer, I have only been here for three days."

You have been here for three years[9] and cannot stay any longer. Listen

*That is to say, when they leave Purgatory.

†The implication is: if you do not, you will return to Earth.

and I shall tell you the reason why! The foul fiend of hell* is coming here tomorrow to seek for prey among us; and as you are handsome and fair, I fear he shall choose you. I would not wish to deceive you for all the gold in the world, and that is why you must come with me."

She led him back to the Eildon Tree, beneath its leafy branches. Huntley Banks was a pleasant place to abide where the birds sang both day and night.

"My falcon has built his nest far, far away from the blue-gray hills, but as he is the prey of the heron, he is unable to stay anywhere. Farewell, Thomas, I shall take my leave through these fields here."

"Fair lady, give me a token† of our meeting so that I may say 'I have known you.'"

She gave him an apple and replied: "Choose, Thomas! You may become the best harpist or the best singer."

"I prefer singing, because speech is of great importance for a minstrel."

"Then I shall make you a gift[10] of a tongue that never lies, and, wherever your feet shall take you, I pray that you shall never speak poorly of me. Farewell, Thomas, I am continuing on my way as I am unable to linger any longer near you!"

Tears flowed from the young man's blue eyes.

"Tell me, beloved lady, if we must leave each other forever?"

"By God, no! Whenever you are in Erceldoune and you take the way of Huntley Banks, I will come to find you if I can."

Mounted on her palfrey, she blew her horn and left Thomas beneath the tree, and this was how they parted.

📖 Murray, ed., *The Romance and Prophecies of Thomas of Erceldoune*; *Thomas of Ersyldoune,* in Laing, ed., *Select Remains of the Ancient Popular Poetry of Scotland,* 137–65.

**Of helle þe foulle fende* (l. 289) refers to the devil, but which one? It is certain that this term overlays another figure.

†*Gyff me a tokynynge* (l. 311), literally, "a tokening."

2. THE SONG OF TANNHÄUSER (LOW GERMAN)

Tannhäuser was a troubadour who lived during the thirteenth century. It may have been his poem known as the Bußlied *("Song of Penitence") which is the source of the legend that appeared in the Germanic regions around 1440 and is distinct from that of Thomas of Erceldoune (also known as Thomas the Rhymer). We have at least five different texts, and many sixteenth-century authors came up with their own versions.*[11] *But the fame of Tannhäuser is due to the composer Richard Wagner (1813–1883), who turned the legend into a three-act opera in 1845, with the plot set in the context of a singing tournament at Wartburg Castle. The fifteenth-century French writer Antoine de la Sale (ca. 1385–ca. 1460) provided another version of the story in his* Le Paradis de la reine Sibylle *(The Paradise of Queen Sibyl).*[12]

I am now going to sing of the wonderful story of the valiant Tannhäuser and the wonders he performed with Lady Venus.

Tannhäuser was an excellent knight who yearned to discover marvels. He wished to enter the mountain of Venus[13] and meet noble ladies there.

"Milord Tannhäuser, I love you!" Venus told him. "Remember that you swore to never leave my side."

"Absolutely not, Lady Venus! I flatly deny that statement, and if someone else told you that, may God help me take my vengeance on him!"

"Milord Tannhäuser, just what are you saying? Stay by my side and I will give you my companions as your women."

"And what would you say if I took another woman, she who occupies all my thoughts! I will be forced to roast in the fires of hell for eternity."

"You talk to me of these fires without ever having felt them. Think instead of my red lips that are forever smiling at you."

"What matter your red lips to me! Give me your permission to leave, for the love of all women!"

"Milord Tannhäuser, if you wish to leave, I shall give you nothing. Stay, noble knight, and keep your life!"

"My life is no longer worth a thing; I cannot remain any longer. Sweet and proud lady, give me your leave!"

"Milord Tannhäuser, don't speak this way anymore, you are out of your mind. Come, let us go into my chamber and play the game of love!"

"Noble and sweet Lady Venus, I believe you are a demoness!"

"What are you saying, Tannhäuser? You are insulting me! You are going to be sorry for this."

"Lady Venus, I cannot remain here a moment longer. Mary, pure Virgin, help me to get away from these women!"

"Milord Tannhäuser, I give you permission to leave. You will sing my praises wherever you go. Rid yourself of the old man!"

Filled with pain and remorse, Tannhäuser left the mountain. "I will go to Rome and entrust myself to the pope. I will follow this path with joy. May God guide my steps until I reach the pope named Urban so that I may learn if he can save me!" he said to himself.

"O Pope, my dear lord, I come to confess to you the great sin I have committed in my life. For the space of one year, I have dwelled in the home of Lady Venus. I would like to confess and expiate my sin in order to learn if God will be able to forgive me." The pope held out a small staff of dead wood.

"If it becomes green with life again," he said, "you shall find divine grace again;[14] it cannot be found any other way."

"If I cannot live even for one year or one day alone upon this earth, I would be able to receive absolution and find consolation from God," Tannhäuser replied.

In despair he left the city. "My pure virgin and mother, I must now leave you!"

He returned to the mountain for eternity.

Lady Venus welcomed him with these words: "Welcome, Tannhäuser, I have long mourned your absence! Welcome my dear lord, the one I love above all others."

Three days later the staff began to turn green so the pope sent his emissaries throughout the land in order to learn where Tannhäuser might be, and to tell him to return, and that God had delivered him from his sins. But he was once again inside the mountain and had found love. This is the reason why Pope Urban was damned for eternity.

Das lyedt dem Tanheuser (1515)[15]

Pope Gregory XI threatened to excommunicate those who tried to visit the Sibylline Mountains, and he had the entrance to the cave there walled up. In the seventeenth century, the Jesuit Martín Del Rio reported that the pope put guards on watch to prevent people from visiting the Sibyl of Norcia. The tale of Tannhäuser corresponds to story type AT 756 C.

📖 Clifton-Everest, *The Tragedy of Knighthood*; Löhmann, "Die Entstehung der Tannhäusersage"; Meier, ed., *Deutsche Volkslieder mit ihren Melodien,* I, 145–61; Ribbeck, *Danuser.*

3. THE TANNHÄUSER OF THE BROTHERS GRIMM (MODERN GERMAN)

The noble Tannhäuser, a German knight, had traveled through many lands and had just come to the Mountain of Venus to see this great wonder. Once he had stayed there for a moment, joyfully and in good humor, his conscience finally compelled him to return to the world, and he asked to take his leave. Lady Venus did all she could to sway him away from his decision.

"I offer as your companion she among my serving maids with the blood-red lips and laughing mouth."

"I desire no other woman except the one who occupies my thoughts. I do not wish to burn in hell for eternity. Her red lips leave me cold as marble. I can stay here no longer for I am withering away."

The she-devil Venus tried to lure him into her chamber to indulge in love play, but the noble knight castigated her and called out to the Holy Virgin until Venus finally allowed him to leave. Haunted by remorse, he took the road to Rome to confess all his sins to Pope Urban and have a penance imposed on him to save his soul. When he confessed that he had spent a whole year in the mountain of Lady Venus, the pope declared:

"When this dead piece of wood I am holding in my hand turns green again, then your sins shall be forgiven."[16]

"Even if I had but a year to live on earth, I would have liked to have felt repentence and performed a penance that would have let God forgive me my sins."

In tears and desperation because of the pope's condemnation, Tannhäuser left the city and returned to the diabolical mountain to live there for eternity. Lady Venus welcomed him with open arms, as one welcomes a long-absent lover.

Three days later, the piece of wood began to turn green with new life, and the pope sent messengers throughout the land to find out where the noble Tannhäuser had gone. But it was too late. He was in the depths of the mountain with the woman he had chosen. There he will remain until Doomsday when God may perhaps send him to another place. No churchman should ever plunge a sinner into despair, but when, full of remorse, he wishes to make atonement, he should pardon him.

GRIMM, *DEUTSCHE SAGEN,* NUMBER 170

4. GUERRIN MESCHINO AT THE HOME OF THE FAIRY ALCINA (ITALIAN)

GVERINO
DETTO
IL MESCHINO.
NEL QVALE SI TRATTA,
Come trouò suo Padre, & sua
Madre nella Città di Du-
razzo in prigione.
Et diuerse Vittorie hauute contra
Turchi.

IN VENETIA, M DC LXXXIX.
Per Andrea Baroni.
Con Licenza de' Superiori.

Andrea de Barberino (1370–1432) wrote this romance around 1410, and twelve manuscripts attest to its popularity. It was published the first time in Padua by Bartolomeo Valdezochio, then in Bologna in 1475 by Baldassarre degli Azoguidi. It was often reworked,[17] *translated in 1530 by Jean de Rochemeure (writing under the pseudonym of Jehan Decuchermoys [Jean de Cuchermois]),*[18] *and became a popular work that was adapted into French and published in 1628.*[19]

Le cinquiesme liure du Mesquin.

Estant Mesquin en la cite de Norsie en Calabre vng viel hôme luy dist quil auoit veu hôme qui auoit este en lieu ou la sibille estoit qui luy auoit dit que les môtaignes ou elle estoit estoiêt toutes plaines de vêtz pource q̃ a merueilles elles sont haultes et y habitent grande quâtite de Griffons & q̃ la plus prouchaine cite ou elle estoit se nômoit Norsie. Mesquin se despartit de Calabre de la cite de Rezio & p ses iournees il arriua en la cite de Norza cheulx vng hoste q̃ beaucoup auoit veu en son têps. Mesquin luy demâda si iamais il auoit ouy pler de la saige Sibille. Lhoste respôdit que il en auoit este biê pres: mais q̃ iamais il ny auoit voulu entrer ne nauoit voulante dy aller. & q̃lle ne demouroit q̃ a troys lieues de celle cite. & que aul- cuns hermites demouroiêt biê pres pour enseigner le chemin a ceulx q̃ vouloient auoient de y aller mais a grât peine les oyseaulx y pouuoiêt voller. & que de ceulx q̃ alloyent il nen retournoit pas vng. La matinee ensuyuante Mesquin alla

The story tells of the wanderings of a young knight in search of his origins. As a child, Guerrin had been kidnapped by pirates and sold as a slave. Once he had grown up, he swore to find his parents again and to travel across the world. During his travels he paid a visit to the Trees of the Sun and Moon, the lair of the Sibyl, and to Saint Patrick's Well, and eventually found his parents.

Upon his arrival in Arezzo, Guerrin asked where the mountain of the fairy (*fata*) Alcina was. An old man heard his question and told him that he owned a book that spoke of this enchantress and two people who had set off to visit her. He recounted the contents of the book: one of the men had died in this place, and the other had lost his courage and turned back. The person who returned from the mountain of the enchantress (*incantatrice*) said that the winds blew violently there and that its peaks were full of griffins.[20]

The city of Norcia* was not far from the mountain, and Guerrin, leaving Arezzo of Calauria,† set off on his journey. He passed by the mountains of Aspromonte,‡ found another huge mountain called Penino,§ and stopped at a nearby inn. The innkeeper was named Anuello. He was a handsome man who was very frank and forthright. He gave him a warm welcome and asked Guerrin where he had come from and where he was going.

"I have traveled the world," Guerrin answered, "and I don't know where I am going."

"Noble gentleman, have I offended you?"

"Not at all!"

"Good! I asked you because I really like to know who comes here."

"Perhaps you have traveled around the world?" Guerrin asked.

"I have gone to Syria, Romania,¶ Spain, England, and to Flanders, and I have visited almost all the countries of the West before returning to my native land, and I can tell you I've known good and evil, and I have discovered the right way one should live in society. When I have a son, I will teach him how to travel and observe."

Guerrin interrogated the innkeeper about the fairy Alcina. Anuello

---

*In Umbria in the province of Perugia. Antoine de la Sale made his way to the Monte della Sibilla (Mountain of the Sibyl) on May 18, 1420, and described his journey in precise detail.

†Arezzo is in Tuscany, so Calauria does not, therefore, refer to Calabria.

‡A mountainous massif of Calabria.

§Perhaps the name of an ancient Roman province, the Alpes Pœninae.

¶Here the term simply refers to a land where a Romance language is spoken.

answered that they were quite close to her mountain but that he had not wanted to go any closer and he did not encourage him to go there. However, if he persisted in his intention, he should know that it was some six miles away, and that there was some sort of fortress near the site, and a little further on, a hermitage. "The hermits advise against and even forbid going beyond," Anuello explained. "Only birds have the possibility to do so because they can fly. There are griffins, eagles, falcons, and other wild beasts. Do not go there, because no one has ever returned."

The next morning, Guerrin asked him if someone could accompany him to town because he wanted to hear Mass, and Anuello gave him his son as a guide. When he was leaving the church, Guerrin spotted some foresters chatting amongst themselves about certain regions and their distinctive features. He joined them and gradually brought the conversation around to enchantments. One of them told him: "Milord, an enchantress named Alcina lives not far from here; she is a virgin that believes God incarnated in her and not in the Virgin Mary.* For this reason, she has been condemned to live in that mountain."

"Is this really true? Who can vouch for this?" asked Guerrin.

An old man, who had been listening to the conversation attentively, replied: "O gentle sir, it is the truth, and I can assure you that this famous fairy remains in our mountain. Three young men have gone there; two returned and the third one vanished. This is the story they told: "There is a hermitage some two miles away, and we did not want to push farther because of the steep cliffs we could see. Two hermits living in this dreadful place own a book that tells of a certain Lionello di Saluzzi di Francia, who boasted of going there. He had not entered the caverns because of the strong winds that blew forth from it and because of numerous obstacles: stones, rock slides, ravines, and cliffs that blocked the path." Guerrin thanked him and invited him to Anuello's inn, which the old man agreed to without a moment's hesitation.

---

*An allusion to the words of the Credo: *Et incarnátus est de Spíritu Sancto ex María Vírgine.*

Deep in thought, Guerrin returned to where he was staying. Toward evening, Anuello sought him out in his chamber and asked: "Why are you so pensive?"

"By my faith, if I could be sure you would keep the secret, I would tell you!"

"Nothing in the world could force me to reveal it," Anuello answered.

"Swear it!" and the innkeeper complied. Guerrin then began to tell him of all his adventures in great detail, which brought his host to tears. Anuello, drying his tears, then said:

"Milord, ask of me what you will, I will do it immediately."

"I am going to leave you my horse and my arms to guard, as well as enough gold and silver to cover two whole years' expenses, especially for treating my noble steed well. Will you do this?"

"Gladly!"

Guerrin was greatly delighted and asked him: "I would like a guide, if possible, to take me to the hermitage."

"None other than I shall serve as your guide," Anuello answered. "But if you want one final piece of advice, do not go there, for the person who makes his way there is no friend of God."

"I can do nothing less in trying to find my father again," replied Guerrin.

"I have heard said that the person who goes there pays for it with his life," Anuello answered back, "but if you persist in your intention, I promise you that I will wait for you for three years instead of the two years you have asked of me."

Guerrin accepted the innkeeper as his guide, and the next day entrusted him with his arms, horse, and a great deal of silver and gold. Anuello had the knight purchase several tallow candles, tinder, and a sack.

After organizing the journey, Anuello brought bread, cheese, and wine for their lunch, and they set out their way toward the cave of enchantments, mounted on two sturdy workhorses. Six miles from

Norcia they came to the castle where they presented themselves to the official* who, on learning of their plans, scolded them sharply and threatened Guerrin with excommunication if he continued on his route. Meschino† informed the official of his intention to find his father, and the other man replied: "Abandon your plan, gentle sir! A person of importance, as you appear to be, is riding to his doom. Only the debauched and the desperate‡ follow this path. And you, Anuello, are you not ashamed to be accompanying him on such a foolhardy undertaking?" Guerrin quickly saw that the official was not wicked and was only speaking to him as a good father would. He therefore answered him this way: "Know that I am not going to the abode of the fairy for any dishonest purpose or to sin, but to find my father, for I have no idea how he is doing, and I think the enchantress can tell me that. My soul is not desperate! Know that in this search for my father I have traveled the world over, visiting India, Asia Major and Minor, Africa, and Barbary. I have been told I should ask the magician Alcina, as she is the only person who can give me this information." The official then had a priest summoned and begged him to take Guerrin's confession. The magistrate then allowed the young man to leave.

This is what Meschino recounted later: "We took the road from the Alps and for four miles labored to cross through difficult territory that was covered with forest. We were forced to walk more often than ride. As evening fell, we found ourselves between two mountainous peaks where the hermitage was located. The sole path ran alongside very steep ravines. It was one mile in length and barely an arm's length in width. Taking it required great attention because it offered a great risk of falling into the abyss. Laboring with our hands and feet we advanced;

*An ecclesiastical judge named by the bishop to handle the business concerning his jurisdiction.

†Il Guerrin Meschino means "the wretched Guerrin."

‡This means those who are in a state of destitution and abandonment, and thought to have lost divine grace. This term recurs constantly in the story of Guerrin Meschino's visit to the home of Alcina.

sometimes we clung to bushes and sometimes to the tops of oaks or boulders. We finally reached the door of the hermitage and knocked on it."

A hermit's voice rang out: "In the name of Jesus of Nazareth, leave!" Another voice exclaimed in tones of great devotion, *"Deus in adiutorium meum intende!"* (O God, come to my aid!)[21] and three hermits then came out singing, each holding a little cross. On spying their two visitors, they urged them to leave: "Back, cursed ones, you who pursue chimeras and illusions! Do you seek to lose your soul and your life?"

"I am the only one who wishes to continue forward, and I am doing so not out of vanity or pride or despair, believe me," Guerrin replied, "but only to learn from what lineage I have been born. I have traveled across the world in vain. The only thing that remains to satisfy my questions is therefore the fairy."

Having listened to them attentively, the hermits[22] turned around to deliberate, then they invited Meschino and Anuello to come in with their horses. "Fathers, don't be of a mind to think I wish to stay here," the latter said. "I have only come as a companion with this gentleman before returning home." Guerrin then told of all his adventures and the monks, moved by his story, said to him: "We beg you to abandon your perilous undertaking; you should place your hopes in God and trust in him rather than risk your life and damn your soul." Meschino heard them out patiently and responded: "I beg you to teach me how to return safe and sound, and save both my life and my soul."

The head of the hermits replied: "Noble gentleman, since you wish not to renounce your plan, whatever it may cost you, I shall give you some instructions—hold them tight in your memory! First and foremost, if you wish to be sure of your salvation, you must keep Jesus Christ constantly in your thoughts. Do not forget to invoke his name, whatever you do, and to honor the four cardinal virtues—strength, justice, temperance, and prudence—as well as the three theological virtues—faith, hope, and charity. Refrain from the deadly sins of envy, greed, and lust, and do not let yourself be swayed by vain and false speech."

"Father," replied Guerrin, "if I manage to gain entry into the home of the fairy, how much time can I remain there?"

"He who enters remains until the sun has achieved one revolution."

"So a day then, right?"

"No! A solar revolution takes place in three hundred sixty-five days, a full year, by traveling through the twelve signs of the zodiac.* Keep this firmly in your memory: when the sun has finished its revolution, you must go out the same way you have entered, otherwise you will be lost and remain in the power of the enchantress."

"Father, give me your blessing," Guerrin asked him. "With it and the grace of God, I hope to return safe and sound."

*In the original text the signs of the zodiac are inserted here with their start and end dates.

He gave confession, took communion, invited the hermits to pray for him, embraced Anuello while reminding him to take good care of his horse and arms, girded his sword at his waist, took provisions of wine and bread that he put into his pack along with tinder and candles, and left.

The path was stony and rutted, surrounded by deep vales and steep cliffs. The mountain peaks were lost in the clouds, and the mountain itself had the shape of a fish from the sea called an aschidor. Light barely penetrated into these ravines, and no tree nor even a blade of grass grew there. It could only be entered during three months of the year, when the sun was in the signs of Gemini, Cancer, and Leo.

When Meschino arrived, the sun was in Cancer, and he carefully observed the area in which he found himself and the most suitable route for him to take. His heart advised him to hurl himself forward and to turn back. Courageously he advanced, tearing his hands on the boulders because the path toward the summit of the mountain was steep and not easy. "I would be better off giving up," he exclaimed, before adding three times: "God, help me!" He soon discovered a passage between two mountains and a footpath he could follow with difficulty.

The path grew wider, and he stopped and found a kind of square place between the high cliffs with an immense mountain directly in front of him. He found that it looked like a cruel and terrible dragon with two immense wings. What he saw in front of him represented the head, and the path he followed, the tail. He eventually spotted the entrance of four dark caves and decided to spend the night where he was, as the sun was vanishing behind the horizon. He recited the seven psalms and other prayers with devotion, and went to bed. On the next day, his sword bared in one hand and a candle in the other, he entered one of these caves and—not forgetting the advice of the hermits—spoke the name of God and requested His aid.

He stepped deeper into the dark cavern and found himself in a kind of dead-end maze and turned back the way he came. As his candle was almost entirely consumed, he appealed for divine assistance. He then spied a small path nearby; he followed it and soon heard something that sounded like a waterfall. When he reached the source of the noise he sat down on a stone near the water's edge, ate a piece of bread, and washed it down with several mouthfuls of wine. Then, feeling drowsy, he took a short nap. When he woke up, he relit his candle, washed himself, made the sign of the cross, and prayed in a low voice. As he advanced through the water[23] he set his foot upon something enormous and soft that was moving, and he barely avoided falling. Once he had gotten past it, he heard: "Who are you, the person who stepped on me? You know that I am condemned to stay in this wet, dark place."

Guerrin felt his hair standing on end, but he was loath to display his fear and grabbed his sword before asking: "Tell me who you are and why you are here?"

"I was judged and condemned to this punishment."

"Where are you from and what is your name?"

"Before I answer you, tell me what you have come here to do." Guerrin Meschino lowered his candle because he wanted to be able to figure out where the voice was coming from. He was greatly stupefied when his eyes fell upon a serpent that was about the length of four arms, and he answered: "You should know, you disfigured and terrifying animal, that I am no knight seeking adventure. I am looking for the fairy Alcina."

"My name is Macco," the monstrous serpent replied, "and for causing harm to my friends and family, I have been condemned to live in this shape. My life was an unbroken series of villainous actions. . . . I let myself become lazy, dove into sin and vice, and was so successful at it that everyone began to hate me and became my enemy. When I heard about this fairy, I decided to pay her a visit to learn if she knew of any remedy for my monstrous condition. After walking about one hundred fathoms, I came to a door, knocked on it loudly, and was told I could not enter because of my great wickedness. I then began cursing the whole of Creation, God, the Virgin, and the saints. Hardly had this curse fallen from my mouth than I found myself changed into a horrible snake, and I am doomed to keep this shape until the Day of the Final Judgment."

"If I prayed to God for you," said Guerrin, "I am certain that it would be a sin because I do not think a more fitting punishment could be inflicted upon you than the one you were given. But who knows, perhaps one day you will find salvation."

"Cursed be you for those words! I would like you to become like me," replied Macco, "and yet I hope that if you persist in going to see the fairy, you will not share my fate."

"Shut your mouth, you miserable wretch! Can't you see that you are damned?"

"Worse!" replied Macco, "my fate is worse than death."

Guerrin drew away from the damned man and soon came across a metal door[24] with the figure of a demon sculpted on either side. It seemed to be alive because its appearance was so terrible. Both of these sculptures held a banner, on which could be read these words: "He who enters here will remain one full year without leaving. He will remain alive until the Day of the Last Judgment, then lose both his soul and his body, and be damned for eternity." After he read this, Guerrin made the sign of the cross over himself, spoke the name of Our Lord three times and gave himself over to His care. Suddenly, three maidens opened the door for him.*

He entered at noon on July 7. The maidens bade him welcome and told him that they had been expecting him. They were very beautiful and so well clad that human language is incapable of describing the magnificence of their garments. The door slammed shut and one of the maidens, with the trace of a fallacious smile, said: "This man shall be our lord!" But Guerrin retorted: "You are fooling yourself." The first maiden took away his bottle of wine, the second his candles and his tinder, and the third, his sword. They then took him by the hand, had

*Note: The illustration reproduced here does not depict the banners that the devils are holding.

him cross through another door, and enter a marvelous garden[25] where stood a tent all covered with decorations, in which there was a group of fifty maidens, each more fetching than the last and all wearing garments sparkling with gold and jewels. Among them he caught sight of one lady whose beauty surpassed that of all the others. A maiden told him: "Milord, this lady you see is the great fairy Alcina." Guerrin Meschino advanced toward her and knelt before her while she bowed back in return while bidding him welcome. They engaged in conversation, and he could see that she was striving to appeal to him as strongly as possible by addressing him with sweet words accompanied by tantalizing gestures. A man less farseeing and less sensible would not have been able to resist the enchantress and would have succumbed to the temptation of such a warm welcome. She had clear skin, a seductive shape, and fascinating speech; he felt troubled but recalled the advice of

the hermits. He said a short prayer, "Jesus Christ, deliver me from these enchantments" three times,[26] and he recovered his wits and all impure desire fled his heart.

To show him that she knew who he was, the fairy told him of all he had endured and added: "I want you to see with your own eyes the treasures I possess." She escorted him into a large, nearby palace and showed him heaps of gold and silver, pearls and precious jewels, which eclipsed all he had known before. She then introduced him into a splendid, luxuriously decorated hall where a group of maidens invited him to join them at a meal brought to them by delectable children.

Once he had eaten and drunk his fill, they led him into a garden that seemed like a new paradise to him. In it were fruits of all kinds. Faced with this abundance, Guerrin had the impression that it was all an illusion because these fruits were not in season.[27]

While strolling about the garden, he asked: "O most wise fairy, how did you come to be damned?"

"I wish for you to know my name." she answered. "The Romans called me Cumana because I was born in the city of the same name, in Campania, and remained in the world one thousand and two hundred years before being judged. When Aeneas came to Italy, I was seven hundred years old, and I led him into the hells; I remained another five hundred years in the temple of Apollo, on the isle of Delphi, during the time of Lucan, Priscian, and Tarquin. During this era, the Romans asked me for laws, and I sent them nine books. Still during this time, thanks to my magic, I asked to remain down here for so long as the world shall last, until the Day of Last Judgment.

"There were ten sibyls, and the best was Erithrea, she who announced that Rome would dominate the world and that the Holy See would rule the city. The first sibyl was Saba the Arab; the second, the queen of Libya; the third, Aftre or Afreica because she was born of sin in the temple of Apollo. Some say this was Cassandra, the daughter of Priam, who announced the destruction of Troy. The fourth was Cipriana, a native of a region near Capua; the fifth was Richea Sachea; the sixth was called Samia; the seventh was me; the eighth bore the name of Hellesponta; the ninth, that of Frigia; the tenth and last, Albunea, was born in Albaturia, a city of Soria. There are many folk who believe that I am dead because, in Sicily, I had a tomb built bearing my name." Guerrin then said: "All-knowing fairy, do you know the fate of my mother and father?"

"Yes! They are still alive, but I will not tell you more for the moment. You must remain here for a year and I will see if I decide to answer you."

She took his hand while talking to him amorously, and invited him to follow her into her palace. Three maidens preceded them—one playing music, the other two singing and miming the acts of love.

A light veil hid the vermillion face of the enchantress, in which two eyes shone like embers burning with love. Guerrin Meschino was invaded by an ardent desire and he forgot the counsels of the hermits. They entered into a room of the palace, the most beautiful he had seen, sat upon the bed and kindled the flame of love with certain touches. The maidens shut the door, Guerrin lowered his eyes and immediately recalled the words of the hermits. He invoked Jesus Christ three times, grew pale, and lost his ardor. He got up, went to the door, opened it, and left. The fairy waited for him, but seeing that he was not coming back, she followed him and asked him why he had left and why he had not given her any pleasure. "Lady, because I am feeling quite poorly," he responded. She believed him, but he could see she was not abandoning her plans to seduce him. He returned to the garden, where many pleasant games were taking place. They then went to dinner and, because he wanted to find his parents, he addressed the fairy tenderly and asked her if she knew where they were.

"They are alive; that I know," she answered. "You never knew them because at the age of two months you were entrusted to a noble lady of Constantinople named Sefferra. Following a series of events, she was forced to flee by sea, but her boat was boarded by the crews of three corsair galleys. Your wet nurse and Seffera were slain. The family that accompanied them was thrown overboard, and you were sold to Epidonio, a merchant of Constantinople. He had a son named Emidonio, whose slave you became. He gave you the name of Meschino, but your baptized name was Guerrin. This is all I am able to tell you." He began weeping and bemoaning his fate, and he kept his resentment a secret so he would be able to obtain more information. His desire to learn the fate of his father remained unsatisfied yet again.

That evening he was led into a rich chamber where, when he was lying by the side of the fairy, she revealed her beauty to him; she unveiled her white skin and her ivory breasts in an attempt to seduce him. He was first caught in the grip of a violent desire, then he made the sign of the cross, but the fairy remained close, trying to achieve her ends. Guerrin remembered the hermits and said to himself: "Jesus of Nazareth, help me!" This invocation was powerful; hardly had he spoken it when the fairy got out of the bed and left the room without knowing what she was doing. Guerrin remained alone and slept peacefully through the whole night without being pestered.

Early in the morning, the fairy came in search of him, accompanied by numerous companions. Once he had risen, he was given a handsome silk garment and a good horse, and he was led out onto a vast plain. This was a Wednesday, and the fairy took him to visit her land. He saw many cities, palaces, and gardens, and she promised he would be the master of all of them. He thought these must be mere images and enchantments because such a limited space as this mountain was not able to hold so many things. He returned to the palace and had all the trouble in the world defending himself against the amorous assaults of the maidens. This temptation lasted until Friday, when he noticed that all the inhabitants of this enchanted land lost their color and vanished.

To his astonishment, over the course of that night he heard great lamentation and the clamor of desperate voices. At sunrise he went out to his balcony and observed that everything was plunged in melancholy and had changed hue. Among the passersby he spotted a man of around forty years of age, letting out painful sighs. He called him over and asked: "Gentle sir, if God does not forbid you, can you tell me why you are changing face and color every minute?"

"Alas, Guerrin," the other replied while hesitating, "for the sake of grace do not add to my torment! If I had known what you were going to ask me, I would never have come here. Do you know what day this is?"*

"Saturday!" Guerrin replied.

"Know that when the pope speaks the Mass, everything found in the fairy's house changes appearance—everyone including men and women, the young and the old, all will become beast, dragon, serpent, basilisk, scorpion, toad, or worm. But you have nothing to fear for they are not able to harm or wound you. Once we have all been transformed, if you are hungry, take pains not to eat in our presence![28] Find a place where you will be alone until tomorrow. We shall remain transformed until the Mass has been said on Monday morning, then we shall regain our human forms. The same thing occurs on every Saturday of the year."[29]

Stupefied, Guerrin questioned him further: "Gentle sir, if this Mass was not celebrated, would all of you remain changed into animals?"

"Yes, because divine Providence had fixed this time limit, but it sometimes happens that the Mass is said sooner and sometimes later."

*The duty to reveal the punishment that strikes the inhabitants of this world on Saturday revives his torments.

Day began to break as they continued conversing. Guerrin asked him what country he was from and why he remained here. With a sigh, the man began cursing the day and hour of his birth and then, while squirming about and tossing his clothing on the path, he began transforming. First the lower part of his body changed into a serpent's tail, like that of a dragon, then the top half of his body and finally the head.[30] Guerrin was completely taken aback by this horrible sight because the creature was the most terrifying thing in the world. He thought to himself: "Even if I have to stay here ten thousand years, I will never commit the sin of the flesh just to avoid being changed into a reptile like this one, with its head a full span in length, barking like a dog, brown in color, as big as a man three arms in length, with eyes of fire, and, when angry, it bites its own tail."

Guerrin saw other similar creatures here—some were larger, some were smaller, all were the color of dirt. He lifted his arms toward heaven and cried: "O Jesus Christ, protect me from this hideous mob!" A short while later, he caught sight of another beast crafted like a toad with its large mouth and four feet. It pressed against its eyes with its forelegs and seemed about ready to explode. Next he saw scorpions that had three mouths for biting and one for eating; they were as big as men and as thin as if they had been left to die of starvation. A little farther away, he could see a kind of worm and numerous black scorpions with bodies similar to a wheel, whose heads were embedded in the ground. Next to these creatures were a number of serpents that had crests on their heads like chickens, and green tails. They were called basilisks, and he thought they looked like the most lecherous beasts he had ever seen: their heads and throats were as red as fire. Soon Guerrin saw even more strange beasts.

Returning to the palace, he found extremely long serpents and vipers that were black on top and white on the bottom, and one of them, which was larger than the others, spoke to him: "Have no fear, I shall not touch you." He found himself something to eat and remained by himself from Saturday evening until the third hour of Monday.

He then left the palace and met the enchantress, who had also been transformed. She was accompanied by wonderfully beautiful maidens. They came to him with their assumed smiles and their beauty paralyzed him. They drew near him to find out what he had learned over the course of the last two days. He greeted them and said to one of them: "O most noble fairy, I ask you if there can be any hope left to me."

"Why do you call me a fairy?" she replied. You are constructed the same way I am. Do you know what our bodies consist of?"

"It contains the four elements," he answered, "water, earth, air, and fire."

"Our bodies are ruled by thirty-four elements and twenty-one of these elements come from nature," she replied. [. . .]*

Guerrin implored her to explain all of this and she told him: "There is first the shape received from the mother and the father, composed and conceded by God, then come five elements. Four of these elements are from the natural order; the fifth is the soul that comes to us from God. When it leaves the body, it returns to its Creator if it has achieved what the common order has commanded it to do in the world. This soul is therefore the fifth element and, when the body is engendered in the mother's womb, it is provided with two companions, one sensitive and one vegetative, like that of the tree.[31] The tree lives but has no feelings, and the same is true for animals. Man possesses the vital, sensitive, and reasonable soul that comes to him from God alone. Animals only have the four elements in their body but have no soul. Without love, the earth would produce no fruits and all would be sterile, for love gives life and movement to all things."

Guerrin acknowledged that this was true and asked: "And the sun?"

"It provides heat, moderates cold and humidity, and makes life possible."

"And Mars?"

*An explanation of the signs of the zodiac is inserted here.

"Mars gives strength to all that lives. The body would not be able to move without this strength."

"And Jupiter?"

"It provides the ability to discern and to know all things."

"What is the case for Saturn?"

"Saturn gives moderation and joy,* this is why melancholy people are called Saturnians."

"Do you know who they are?"

"They are born when Saturn is in Pisces, a wet, cold, and heavy sign. If Saturn did not provide these dispositions, the human body would be so volatile that the world could not last, for it would have no foundation."

When the fairy stopped talking, Guerrin prompted her to continue.

"There are five senses and sentiments in the body: sight, hearing, touch, taste, and smell. When one of them is missing, the body is crippled. The other three are memory, intelligence, and will. They are the thirty-four rulers of the body."

"Noble lady," said Guerrin, "we have one more, free will, which comes to us from God."

"What is that?" she asked.

"It is the freedom we have to do either good or evil, and we shall be judged in accordance with our actions."

"If this true, why haven't you left, as you have spent eight days with me?"

"Because I was told that I would not be able to leave until the end of the year," replied Meschino, which caused the fairy to laugh.

Then Guerrin asked: "O most noble fairy, why were those people that I saw transformed into different kinds of reptiles?"

"I am going to tell you, but first tell me what you saw."

"I saw a handsome man turn into a terrifying dragon that had seven horns on its head."

**Saturno gli da temperanza e allegrezza, però questi sono chiamati corpi malinconici Saturnini.* This joy is in contradiction with melancholy!

"When he was still in the world, he was a minor lord living in the mountains of Calauria. He was full of pride and full of the seven deadly sins and was waging war constantly against his neighbors, which brought about the death of his wife. He came here, full of despair, to flee his enemies. I am not permitted to tell you his name. Some claim that he died in a brawl, but his body was never found because he was condemned to be changed into a beast because of his sins. The seven horns represent these sins."

"I saw another kind of worm, which was three fathoms long, with a small head, glowing eyes, and a horse's tail. It was biting its own tail and its color made it resemble a viper."

"That was a bad-tempered man, who was always getting carried away."

"I also saw other ugly, vile reptiles, swollen like toads to the point of exploding."

"Those are the envious."

"I saw worms that resembled very large scorpions that had three mouths for biting and one, which was much larger, for eating."

"They are those who are avaricious and miserly toward their parents, God, and the poor. In fact, avarice is only a form of self-harm because you love neither God nor your family.* These individuals were so avaricious that they despaired and ended up here."

"I saw another kind of worm," Guerrin continued, "they were a kind of hideous black scorpion with bodies in the shape of wheels and their heads buried in the ground."

"Those are the lazy who are hateful, ill-intentioned, and envious; that is why they have come to ruin here."

"I have seen snakes who gave off a great stench and had their mouths open as if they wanted to eat."

"Those are the people who committed the sin of gluttony."

"Moreover, I have seen a kind of worm with a green tail, wings like serpents, a comb like [that of] chickens, and glowing eyes."

---

*Avarice is one of the seven deadly sins, defined from interpretations of Saint Augustine's writings on the genealogy of sin. It is the opposite of charity that comes from pride. Cf. Augustine, *De Genesi ad litteram,* XI, 15.

"Those are ones who were overcome by lust and were greatly criticized and threatened for it. They despaired* and decided to seek refuge here."

By these words, Guerrin realized that they were all subject to divine justice until the Day of the Last Judgment because they had committed the seven deadly sins.[32]

Shortly after he had grasped the reason for the transformation of the men into different kinds of serpents, he thanked God and prayed to Him that he grant him the grace of leaving this place safe and sound, to find his mother and father, and finally to save his soul. It is not unlikely that he was strongly tempted by lust this week, but he always turned to God, who helped him. Every morning he recited the seven psalms and other prayers. This was how another week went by during which he once again witnessed the metamorphoses described above.

When everything returned to normal, he begged the fairy to tell him where his father was. She was disposed to satisfy his request on condition he indulge in lustful play with her. But he held his silence and did not answer. She grew angry, and the entire year went by without them seeing one another.

Three days remained before the end of the year, and the fairy had been changed into a reptile as determined by divine justice. Guerrin, wondering how to know the fate of his parents, felt overwhelmed and decided to turn again to the fairy. Once she had resumed her human shape, he questioned her: "O most learned fairy, I pray you to reveal the past, particularly what has become of my parents so that my quest will not have been in vain."

"I regret I ever told you that you were of noble lineage because you

---

*Despair is considered to be the sin of dereliction, and the text uses *accidia* (acedia, "apathy, spiritual or mental sloth"), which, in theological Latin, represents a deadly sin. In his *Summa Theologica,* Saint Thomas Aquinas describes the outline of the seven deadly sins by means of the theory of the five faculties of the soul dear to Aristotle (vegetative, sensitive, locomotive, appetitive, intellective). Acedia is an aversion toward God himself and the things connected with him, a loss of faith, doubting the redemption, and the doubt that leads to despair. For more on this, see the study by Wenzel, *The Sin of Sloth: Acedia in Medieval Thought and Literature* (1967).

are a very poorly educated knight," she answered, full of rage.

Vexed by this response, Guerrin lost his temper: "I beseech you to answer me by virtue of the leaves you place upon the altar that do not fly away when the wind blows."*

Alcina replied: "Duke Aeneas was more noble than you when I guided him through hell and showed him his father Anchises. He informed him that he had founded Rome as had been prophesized by Carmenta, the mother of King Evander.[33] You must remain for yet three more days, no more, otherwise something bad will happen to you. I repeat, neither I nor any other person can give you any knowledge about the fate of your parents."

Wishing to find them, Guerrin checked his wrath and promised he would speak of nothing but her nobility and beauty, and would hide her transformation into a horrible reptile from everyone. She responded: "Honor, shame, wealth, and parents matter little to me because, to satisfy my appetite, I abandoned God." At the sight of this tough stance, the angry Guerrin erupted: "O renegade fairy, cursed by God for all eternity,[34] I implore you by the divine power of the Father, the Son, and the Holy Ghost to tell me where my father is, as you certainly know it!"

"O false Christian, your incantations cannot harm me because I am not supernatural.[35] Instead, go beseech the demons that possess no bodies, and the unclean spirits! Go to the very end of the West Wind, look for hell, and you shall be shown the image of your father!"

Terrified by these words, Guerrin feared he would only find his father again when he was dead, suffering the torments of hell.[36] He spoke not a word, but bolstered his heart against ill fortune and replied: "By the grace of God, that is not how it shall be! Have everything I brought into this cursed place returned to me." She had his sack with

*An allusion to the way in which the sibyl predicted the future by using leaves. Jean de Rochemeure writes: "par la vertu des feuilles q souloyêt auoir celles q tu fitz sur laultier de almeno qui par tousiours en leurs entiers demeuroient en demonstrant ta vraye prophetie" (by the virtue of the leaves that you placed on the altar of Almeno, which always remain whole and reveal the true prophecy).

its two loaves of bread, tinder, phosphorus, and a candle to replace the one that had already been burned, given back to him, and said: "Don't think that your anger can harm me or offend me, because no mortal can do me good or ill; I must remain just as I am," and she left.

The next morning he recited the seven psalms and other prayers, again requested the help of Jesus Christ, and set off in search of the door he had come in by, without managing to find it. He grew scared and commended himself to God so that he would not perish because he felt he was in a huge labyrinth that was darker than the one in Crete where the Minotaur devoured the Athenians awarded him by the judgment of Minos.

The last day arrived and, at the ninth hour, a maiden came up to Guerrin and said: "O knight, forget not that the divine power compels us to tell you when you can leave and where to find the exit." Guerrin rejoiced and praised God. She took him through a courtyard that he had not seen for a full year. The maiden told him that if he wished to stay, she would take care of things so that the fairy would forgive him. She tried to deceive him but Guerrin told her he would rather die than be damned.

"O noble Guerrin," she replied, "know that during your stay in these places you have gone beyond the threshold of death, your death was impossible because no one can die here before Doomsday.

"Nothing will happen to me," he responded, "because the charity, faith, and hope I have in Jesus Christ will keep me safe and sound. I prefer to place all my hope in God than to remain in this infamous place. Open the door for me!"

She hesitated a little longer and then complied with his request. "Tomorrow I will go to see Macco, who has been changed into a horrible reptile," Guerrin said before leaving. Once he had stepped through the door, he heard the maiden yelling to him: "You will never succeed in finding your parents!" Looking back, Guerrin retorted: "Go and tell the fairy Alcina that I am alive and healthy, that I will attain my purpose while saving my soul, and that I will not live one more day of this sinful, criminal life that causes your transformation into evil, mindless beasts," which made her laugh.

He then set off into the darkness, and when it seemed he had come close to Macco, he began saying: "Jesus of Nazareth, protect me." He thought he could hear a hundred voices howling in pain, sad to see him leaving. Macco asked him: "What do you want of me?"

"Macco, when I am once again back in your city, what news would you have me bring?"

"I beg you to say neither good nor ill of me."

"Do you hope to get out of here?"

"No. I am waiting for the Day of Last Judgment that will be for me a second death and a second punishment."

"Thus, you are already dead once and you are waiting for a second death?"

"I am not dead, but find myself in more evil straits than if I was, because I must atone for my laziness."

"Why don't we both leave this place of darkness?"

"I cannot because the Divine Judge has condemned me to remain here until the trumpet of the Last Judgment sounds. We shall then die and be judged."

"Don't you feel any love for God or for any other creature?"

"We have no love in us,[37] quite the contrary! We carry hatred and envy within us. I am delighted to think that you have bravely traveled across the world in search of your parents at the cost of much pain and fatigue, but that you were vanquished by a most iniquitous woman.[38] Your departure intensifies my anger and my torments."*

"Your pain will increase even more because I am going to go to Rome to confess to the holy pope, repent for my sins, and take communion while you will still remain in this horrible place. I am going to have you excommunicated!"

It is impossible to describe the darkness and shadows of the cavern formed from red stone, which was sometimes narrow because of rockslides and sometimes quite wide. There were ravines everywhere on the

*Because Guerrin had not sinned and therefore could leave the world of the fairy.

mountain. He walked here and there in search of the cave entrance, fearing that his candle would be used up and he would have no more light, for then he would be truly lost. Strength of arms was useless to him here, so he placed his hope in God and offered Him his prayers. It was precisely at this moment that he found the exit; it was midnight. His candle went out that very instant and he was lost in darkness. The moon was in the sign of Scorpio and the sun was in that of Cancer, and the night was darker than usual. He made the decision to sleep for a while and wait for the coming of dawn to resume his journey.

The next day he made his way back to the hermitage where he had left Anuello and the three hermits. All gave him a very warm welcome. He took a seat, and asked that his horse and weapons be returned, then he ate and drank the wine Anuello had brought for him. Once he had gotten comfortable, the hermits asked him about his adventure. He told them of all he had seen and experienced, and told them of Macco and his punishment. They advised him to go see the pope, who alone had the power to absolve him, as all those who resided at the fairy's home had been excommunicated.

He mounted his horse and returned to Norcia with Anuello, then thanked him, left him his arms, gold, and silver, placed himself in God's hands, and left for Rome, where he arrived in a few days. He rested for a day in an inn before making his way to Saint Peter's where he asked to speak to the pope, but he had to wait for three days before getting an audience along with the ambassadors.

While asking for mercy, he knelt at the feet of the pope and while bemoaning his lot, told him: "Most Holy Father, have pity on me because there is no greater sinner on the earth than me." The sovereign pontiff asked him to explain. Guerrin told him his story and how he had spent an entire year at the dwelling of the fairy. He went on to tell the pope: "In Constantinople I was called Meschino, but the trees of the sun told me that Guerrin was my name."

"Are you the one that fought a great battle again King Astiladoro?"[39] the pope asked.

"Yes!"

The pope blessed him and added: "Ask of me what you will." Guerrin reported what the three hermits had told him when he went to visit the enchantress Alcina's home, and he gave him the letter that they had written in which all this had been copied down.

"As it was to find your father, I give you my blessing," said the pope while placing his hand on Guerrin's head. "As penance for going to the fairy's house and for visiting the idols of the trees of the sun,[40] I command you to go to Saint Patrick's Purgatory* in Hibernia, to Santiago de Compostela, and to Santa María of Fisterra. Once you have performed this penance, Jesus Christ shall absolve you. After you have been to Saint Patrick's Purgatory, if you are of a mind to do so, please come back to tell me of what you have seen."

"O Holy Father, I am going to obey you, but I have no money."

The pope had two hundred ducats given him while he advised him to beware of robbers on the Way of Saint James. Guerrin returned to his inn and, on the next day, he left Rome.

This took place in the year of our Lord 824, during the papacy of Pope Benedict Eugenius II, when Charlemagne was emperor.

ANDREA DE' MAGNABOTTI DA BARBERINO, *GUERINO MESCHINO* (EDITION OF 1689), BOOK V, CHAPTERS 136–54[41]

📖 Babbi, "Le traduzioni del *Guerrin Meschino* in Francia," "Le *Guerrin Meschino* d'Andrea da Barberino et le remaniement de Jean de Rochemeure," and "Jean de Rochemeure, traduttore del *Guerrin Meschino*"; Montorsi, "Le *Guérin Mesquin,* traduit par Jehan de Cucharmois 'natif de Lyon'"; Ueltschi, "Sibylle, Arthur et Sainte Agathe."

*Located on the island of Lough Derg (Donegal).

part two

Romances of Adventure

four

Duke Ernst

(*Middle High German*)

Written around 1190, Herzog Ernst *(Duke Ernst) is an adventure romance consisting of 6,022 short verses. Its popularity lasted into the twentieth century. In 1819 Ludwig Uhland wrote a theatrical play based on* Herzog Ernst, *and Karl Simrock used it as the basis for a popular book. In 1955, Peter Hacks wrote a drama using this story. This is also one of the rare texts that was translated into Latin several times and was transformed into a lay during the fifteenth century.*[1] *Its success can be explained by the fact it introduced several motifs into the literature of*

entertainment, such as the peoples from the ends of the earth, and this was also the romance in which "crane-men" (creatures with human bodies and birds' heads) first appeared.

After he was exiled from Germany by his father-in-law, Kaiser Otto, Duke Ernst made his way to Constantinople where, with the aid of the Greeks, he headed off for the Holy Land.[2]

1. HOW THEY ARRIVED IN THE LAND OF GRIPPIA

After taking their leave of Basileus, they set sail, accompanied by five Greek ships, and set a course for Syria. Five days later a terrifying storm blew in and scattered the boats. Twelve were destroyed completely with no survivors. The duke's ship was blown so far off course that he lost sight of the other vessels and agonized about the loss of his Greek knights. The wind continued to drive his boat further and further away. By good fortune, Ernst had gathered together on his vessel all the bold German knights who owed him allegiance. After sailing for more than three months on a raging sea, a sea on which no man had ever sailed before, Ernst began to despair because the food stores were exhausted and everyone thought they were going to die.

One fine morning at dawn, the sky cleared and good weather returned. The sky was blue, the sea was peaceful, and the wind had calmed. The knights spotted a country called Grippia, toward which they aimed their ship. They entered a port and dropped anchor on a solid seabed. They saw a magnificent city girded by solid walls of yellow, green, blue, black, and red marble, decorated with both common and strange images that are impossible to describe. The ramparts had been constructed by the hands of a master and adorned with gold and a variety of gems, both small and large. A feeling of power emanated from this city: it feared no assault because its towers and defenses were so skillfully constructed. Singular individuals lived in this city.

When the bold warriors approached, they lowered the sails and dropped anchor immediately, and put a small boat into the water. Ernst then said to his friends and companions: "It seems to me that divine Providence has guided us to this beautiful land up to this magnificent city so we can procure food before we die of hunger. When we were sailing at sea with no possibility of landing anywhere, we went through some hard times. Now that we have discovered this splendid city, I presume its inhabitants guard it. We are going to see if they are Christians or heathens, and behave cautiously to obtain whatever food they will sell us. If they are heathens, they will not let us set off again safe and sound. It matters little if we lose our lives here as we have departed for the Holy Land! Better to fall in these places than to perish of hunger on the boat."

The knights echoed his statement. "Yes, we left on pilgrimage without any other intention!" They were ready to die in the service of God and tolerate joys and pains for His glory. The bold and noble knights carefully donned their shining armor. Once they were armed, they got into the boat. Upon landing, the duke raised a red banner that he ordered Count Wetzel to carry. The count bravely took the lead of the band and led it to the gates of the city where all came to a halt. The gates were wide open, yet the valiant knights could not see anyone on the ramparts, which was a huge surprise to them. "These are very strange folk that dwell here," the duke said. "They do not show themselves. What could this mean? I think they are hiding to avoid us. They want to draw us into the city so they can easily overcome us when we enter. There could be no other reason for why they are not showing themselves. They should be careful; they could easily run into a streak of misfortune. Before they can kill us, we should be able to cut a good number of them to pieces because we are well equipped with our solid cloaks of shining chain mail! Gather together, young knights, cross the drawbridge and enter the city with the banner at your head! Before they realize it and hunt us down, we shall have knocked in their defenses. Bold heroes, prepare yourselves so that the inhabitants of this fortress will retain the memory of this battle in their very flesh!"

With determination and courage, these seasoned fighters grouped around the banner firmly held by the valorous Count Wetzel, who led them into the city. No one opposed their advance; they quickly made their way inside without anyone appearing[3] and, ever vigilant, made their way into the very heart of the city without having had to engage in battle. The knights discovered a verdant garden that was fresh at all times, and a round palace, called *würmelage*[4] in the common tongue, with many chairs. They then saw many tables arranged in a circle, covered in silken tablecloths with magnificent gold borders. No emperor was ever rich enough to find a seat there. The chairs were equally as handsome. The tables were artfully set, I can tell you, and covered with meats, game, bread, fish, mead, blackberry wine and other wines, the best that I have ever drunk. The cups and plates were made of gold, and the platters were all engraved silver. The knights found everything they needed there. Ernst told them: "The most sensible thing is to eat, but let us not forget to thank God from the bottom of our hearts for what he has so generously provided us today. We can take without sin the food that we find, but touch not the rest! God perhaps wishes to lead us into temptation. Do not covet the gold or jewels of the inhabitants, or their rich fabrics. Praise the Lord for he has often protected us and procured us this food! Never has our need for food been greater. Without His help, we would have died of hunger amidst the wild waves—shamefully without a fight. God has miraculously saved us! Sit at the table and eat joyfully so that you may be reinvigorated! Next, follow my counsel and quickly load our boat with provisions for the voyage to Jerusalem. We cannot remain here past daybreak, so we will hoist our sails. I have seen that this city is not completely abandoned; its inhabitants are surely not far away. We should expect that they will return soon."

The knights then went to wash their hands. These bold knights sat down at the tables and ate and drank until they were sated. They all then got up and strolled about the city, carefully looking at the many treasures of gold, precious stones, and exquisite jewels. They eventually came to a house where, thanks to divine Providence, they found meat, wine, and bread in such huge quantity it cannot be imagined. There was enough to feed a king and his entire army! Their jubilation was great and they immediately provisioned their boat. They remained on board to rest, leaving the beautiful city wide open and empty. After resting for a moment, the duke suddenly said to Count Wetzel: "I have a great desire to return to take a closer look at this city, whatever may happen. It is certainly well laid out. If you want to come with me, tell me so now!"

"Gladly," Wetzel replied. "Have no worries about my life, milord! Let us ask our companions, however, if they wish to respect the principles of chivalry, to stand ready to give us aid, to charge if they see us attacked, and to be ready to courageously step in if they hear the din of combat so as to rescue us in time. The city is extensive, and I find it hard to believe that it has no inhabitants. If we accept the fact that they do not want to show themselves, it is because they want to see what we are going to do. Even if they are not attacking us, we should really discover what their plans are. May God help us!"

The knights promised that they would fight or die with him.

On their return into the city, they discovered masterpieces in gold and were able to admire all kinds of amazing objects studded with gems; they saw many remarkable palaces skillfully constructed, arcades, large doors shining like stars and decorated in a way seen nowhere else. Everything that had been built here, both inside and outside, had been executed by the hand of a master. Inside they found luxurious halls and chambers. This sumptuous city was so close to the coast that even a powerful king would have abandoned the idea of attacking it with his army if that had been his intention. After contemplation of these wonders, they continued their exploration. They discovered another palace not far from the spot where they had dined earlier. It was plated with gold, and the walls were sparkling with emeralds. The duke entered a grandiose chamber, ornamented with gems set in shining gold, and in it he found a bed inlaid with gold and pearls, and on the frame of which were lions, dragons, and serpents in beaten gold. [. . .][5]

After the brave warriors had admired all these riches, they went out and found themselves in a beautiful courtyard planted with cedars. They drew closer and discovered two springs, one with hot water the other with cold. They were designed in such a way as to flow parallel to one another and they babbled pleasantly. Right next to them were baths made entirely of green marble, topped by a vault supported by flying buttresses, and two bathtubs of red gold fed by two silver pipes—can you imagine anything more beautiful?—that brought in running water that was hot or cold, depending on what was desired. This entire system was very skillfully contrived. As I had heard someone say, the water flowed out of the bathtubs through a bronze pipe that crossed through the entire city. The dwellers of this city had thought of everything. The streets and alleys were paved with marble green as grass, and when they needed to be cleaned, the water was allowed to flow all over the city, which got rid of all the waste and dust. In this way, in the space of an instant, everything was clean and the streets sparkled like snow. I believe no more beautiful city ever existed in the world.*

When Ernst had seen all these wonders, he said to Count Wetzel: "Brave companion, I feel a real desire to take a bath. Let us do so without fear! I believe there is no one here who can do us harm. If the opposite proves to be true, we will know it immediately and be ready to defend ourselves. We have survived all the perils of the sea and truly deserve this break."

"Since you have no desire to abandon your intention, I am going to follow you, but reluctantly. Because you seem to wish to know nothing, I will also take a quick bath. However, you should be aware that our situation gives me fear of being slain here without being able to fight."

Thereupon they took off their clothes and sat inside the bathtubs that they filled with hot and cold clear water, which they enjoyed greatly. Once they had bathed, they left the premises to avoid any unpleasant

*The fascination of the author is palpable as he describes an Oriental palace that is the exact opposite of what could be found in the West during this time.

encounters. Since they saw no one, they returned without hesitation to the chamber of the splendid palace in which they had seen the beautifully decorated bed earlier. They lay down in it to get some rest, something that would bring them misfortunes later.

After a short while, Count Wetzel said to the duke: "It is time to return to our ship and companions. They must certainly be worried about what may have happened to us and the time we have been away must seem long to them. Let us get dressed so we may be able to defend ourselves if called upon to do so. We have seen all the splendors of this city and can state without lying that we have never seen anything more beautiful."

The two knights armed themselves without any further delay. They had grabbed their shields and were leaving the palace when they heard strange voices in front of the city. These were strange and powerful voices as if wild cranes were calling from all over. Never before had they heard such a din! In great surprise, Ernst and Wetzel leaned out of a window that overlooked the garden. Their gaze embraced the entire city, and they could see without being seen. They remained on the lookout because no one could approach them without being seen. After they had lingered a moment, they suddenly caught sight of a strange troop of men and women in front of the city gates.

All of these individuals were well formed, both young and old, but with necks and heads like those of cranes.*[6] Our knights watched them coming closer. The only weapons these beings carried were shields, bows, and quivers filled with terrifying arrows. Their clothing was made of precious silk and velvet, and embroidered in gold and silk, according to personal taste. With the exception of their overlong necks, these people exhibited no imperfections.

Men and women alike were solidly built and vigorous. The city belonged to them; they were proud, bold, and happy to be alive. They were rich in gold and silver, and each individual had as much as he or

*This is the first time that crane-men appeared in medieval literature.

she wished. Moreover, they had significant revenues and were subjects of a king. This king had gone to India with his army and many boats. He had slain the sovereign of this country just when the latter was getting ready to flee with his wife because he could not defend himself. He sunk the boat that the queen was on. Only their daughter survived; her beauty saved her life. The powerful monarch of Grippia,* the king of the crane-men, wanted to marry her and bring her back to his home. It was in her honor that the feast had been prepared and all the inhabitants of the city had gone to welcome their arrival on their shores in a state of euphoria. Accompanying the fiancée, these strange men had come to the gates of the city where its inhabitants, adorned in their best finery, had gathered to welcome them. When Ernst and Wetzel had sufficiently observed these peculiar people, they felt no great fear, for they did not think very much of them.

"I would like to remain here a little longer," said Ernst. "Even if they seek to prevent us, we will be able to return to our ship. Here this evening we shall be able to learn their intentions. They wish to celebrate and feast; the dishes we found were prepared for them. They left everything out without any concern."

*Grippia is a contracted version of Colonia Agrippina, the former name of Cologne.

"Milord, I am your* vassal, and you can count upon my loyalty. You may be sure that I am ready to risk my life and all I own for you. These folk cannot oppose us with their mediocre weapons, and even if they had a larger army, it would not scare me. Whether there were a thousand of them or more, I would take them on single-handedly! If they attacked me en masse, I would carve a path through them with my sword. Know that I would give them no quarter! We are seasoned warriors, and if we dodge their arrows, we could in very short order, if I am not mistaken, inflict such losses on them that they would forget all about their bows and we would decapitate more than one of them. Their necks are so slender it would be a huge massacre if they attacked us. It is here, in their own fortress, that we will learn if they are true warriors."

They saw two men enter side by side who were richly dressed in clothing with silken embroidery, over which they wore two tricolored robes. Their linen pants were white as snow, and hanging from them were gold ribbons that were cut and split as was proper at court. They each wore a pair of gold spurs on their heels. These two men, selected from among the best, preceded the king with a haughty and solemn march. From shoulder to head they looked like cranes. Each of them carried a splendid white ivory quiver whose sides were inlaid with precious stones, a bow of horn, and a gold shield the boss of which was shaped like an almond and had an unsurpassable glow.† Two other figures followed them who were dressed with equal luxury. Ernst and Wetzel saw that the king wore a crown covered with precious stones. However, he also had the neck and the head of a swan.‡ He had chosen two of the great men of the kingdom to escort the most beautiful woman the world had ever seen. [. . .] She was weeping copiously and sadly walking beneath a canopy that gave her shade and lessened the

*The informal and the formal terms of address are used interchangeably here.

†Amandine or alabandine is a gemstone that owes its name to Alabandina, which is another name for Ephesus. It is a sparkling red in color. It expels all poisons, gives the gift of prophecy, allows the wearer to interpret dreams, and confers invisibility.

‡The swan is nobler than the crane, hence this comparison.

heat. She was born in India from where the king had abducted her as I described earlier. The simultaneous deaths of her mother and father had deeply affected her. All the inhabitants entered after her, singing a strange melody in their language. The fiancée was brought into a beautiful chamber and the festival began. The king had the princess take a seat. She continued lamenting not seeing around her anyone capable of understanding her or speaking to her. This is why, visible to all, endless tears rolled down her face to her chest. She was wearing black because she was in mourning. Even if these people resembled humans, she was incapable of understanding them: she heard only their calls and tried to communicate with gestures.

With his wand, the seneschal indicated where everyone should sit at the table; only the servants remained standing to serve the wine. The king of Grippia took his seat in a dignified manner with the beautiful maiden seated by his side. They were offered water in golden basins to wash their hands; kneeling valets handed out napkins that were white as snow. Mead or wine was poured into large golden goblets. The seneschal then discovered that the dishes prepared earlier had vanished; he ordered his servants to go to the kitchen at once for more. So many were brought out that finally no one had any worries about where the earlier dishes had gone: the guests believed that their own people had eaten them. Meats were offered and everyone celebrated except the charming maiden who took no part in the general merriment. The king kissed her, often slipping his beak into her mouth and she had to suffer these signs of love that were unknown in India. Her eyes were red with weeping and she could not confide her distress to anyone. Duke Ernst caught sight of her sorrow and was moved to see her in such despair.

"If we do nothing to rescue this beautiful princess from these people," he said, "I will regret it for the rest of my life. Think, my friend, of a way we might be able to assist her. What misfortune if this beautiful maiden must remain in this strange land until the end of her days! If you agree, and putting ourselves in God's hands, I would like to slip into this room with our swords drawn to surprise them. We will slaughter them like animals; we will drown them in their own blood! They have naught but arrows. How can they have any effect against our armor? We will pierce through them until we reach the young lady, free her, and slay the king. We will take the princess out safe and sound before they can mount a counterattack. And even if their army was even more powerful, we would still manage to get out of the city. Follow me, bold knight!

"Hear my advice," replied Count Wetzel, "let's not act too hastily! I will follow you, whatever the cost, but you have seen how many they are. If we wish to keep our lives, we must think before attacking because there is a risk they will kill the princess. It will be easier to help her at the moment they are leaving the table and all the warriors have gone into the garden together. We can then enter the chamber, slay the king immediately, and take the princess out. Before they have even realized what has happened, we will have made our way to the gates of the city where our companions will come to our rescue. Under our protection, we will lead the maiden to our ship; this is how I see things."

The two knights did not have long to wait. Once the meal was over, all rose and the king went into the large hall. People danced and sang to the sound of music; calls and cries could be heard that were like those of cranes and herons. This was how they were paying homage to the king's fiancée, but no matter what they did, the princess did not cheer up and the monarch took umbrage. He ordered everyone to leave because he wanted to enter the nuptial chamber where the maiden had been taken. The guests all returned to their homes. The only ones remaining with the king were his most important vassals whom he kept with him always to advise him. They were in the chamber where the fiancée was to be undressed. A servant spied the two armed knights in a corner and immediately returned to the chamber and reported it. The Grippians thought they must be hostile Indians and took fright. They immediately attacked the beautiful princess in revenge, pecking her all over with their beaks causing her to cry out in pain. Ernst and Wetzel flinched, and wrath took hold of them. "We should have already gone to her aid; she is proclaiming her distress. They most certainly have slain her, but now they are going to feel the weight of our vengeance!" They rushed the chamber unsheathing their swords, slew the king and his people. No one escaped except the one who had informed the others of their presence, and he just barely got away. He fled when he heard the clash of steel and rushed away to spread the news throughout the city, and the people made a great clamor.

The duke bowed to the princess and greeted her. "Your sad fate awoke my pity. By God, they will pay for what they've done. Tell, me fair maiden, how may I help you? If God had granted me the grace to save you, have no doubt that I would have led you onto my boat with my knights. If you are doomed to die, please know that I will wreak such vengeance on your enemies that it will leave them scarred for the rest of their lives. Our reprisals will be so fierce that they will still be talking about it ceaselessly to their descendants."

The king of India's daughter was bathed in her own blood and could not move because she was in her death throes. Her heart began to break and she grew weaker, but told the duke: "Noble knight, may God reward you for the pains you took for me and the danger you have met in this strange land. Whatever becomes of me, I praise God for sending you to help and console me; you have spared me the numerous sufferings that a marriage like that would have given me. If God wishes my health to be restored, you will rejoice because of it, and if He helps you to accompany me back to India, and if you wish to stay there, noble and valiant knight, I will entrust you with supreme power and great honors, and you will be the equal of kings. My father had many vassals who served him irreproachably and assisted him in any and all battles, and whom he rewarded with gold. Know that I am his only daughter, and the crown comes to me by right. But fate has decided otherwise, and I must remain in this strange land until the Day of the Last Judgment. But death is sweeter to me than the prospect of spending my whole life in such despair. May God grant you to find your way back home safe and sound!"

She bowed before the duke and the moment her voice went quiet, her soul fled her body. Moved by great emotion, Ernst and Wetzel mourned the death of the princess. They laid her down on a bier and prayed Our Lord to take her into His kingdom, and they then left the palace.

Warriors were blocking the exit, and they found themselves encircled on all sides. With a loud roar the crane-men set upon the duke and the count, who were unable to escape. They had to carve a passage through their adversaries with their swords, cutting through their long slender necks and not sparing anyone. This was how they made their way to the city gate, which was locked. They put their backs against the wall to defend themselves. Arrows were shot at them from all sides. It was the only way they could be attacked. The weight of the arrows stuck in their shields made it almost impossible to carry them. The valiant knights tore them out and stamped on them. They were in such peril that their very lives were at risk.

Their companions on the boat could hear the clash of arms. Following their banner, they rushed to the rescue, brandishing their long, sharp swords and, without delay, forced open the gates to the city where they leaped into the fray, which saved the two noble knights. More than one of them lost their lives in this assault. They then had to avoid the rocks thrown from the ramparts as the duke and his retinue beat a retreat; they managed to escape without suffering any further losses. This was all a high price to pay for a visit and a bath! They headed toward their ship, intimidated and under duress, but relieved at the same time. It was then that the duke and his men suffered a great fright: while heading back toward their ship, the brave warriors suddenly spotted a formidable army made up of the nobles of the country who had come to see the fiancée. The Christians estimated their number at twelve thousand: they were well-equipped and imposing. They were riding the most handsome steeds in the world and carrying horn bows. They went on the attack.

Duke Ernst then told his companions: "Today, you will have to show proof of your valor! As they have cut off our route leading to the ship, gather around our banner and defend yourselves like gallant knights! We will pay for passage to the kingdom of heaven and eternal bliss with our lives. These folk are heathens who have no respect for God. Turn your hearts toward Our Lord so that He will grace us with His aid. Knights, have no fear of death!"

Following this exhortation, they all readied themselves for battle, as bold heroes should do. The duke grabbed the banner and took the lead of his troop. The knights attacked them enthusiastically, loosing countless arrows against which armor and shield were useless. The Christians were surrounded and could not strike back at the heathens, who kept their distance. The duke realized that the enemy refused to fight on foot, and many knights lost their lives in this relentless battle. They drove their way through the opposing army until they reached the sea. There the knights defended themselves until the sailors arrived in their boat, which then took them back to the ship. They headed out into the open sea, and God sent them the best of winds to their great relief, although they were sorrowful about having to leave their dead behind.

Under full sail, they sailed into unknown waters while the heathens, furious at the losses they had suffered, vainly tried to catch them in their swift galleys. But the pilgrim knights left death behind them; they experienced much suffering while at sea and were thereby washed of a number of their sins.

2. THE MAGNETIC MOUNTAIN

The story tells us, that twelve days later, the current carried them to a land where stood a gigantic mountain that was called the Magnetic Mountain.[7] You can imagine their hope on seeing that land! They then saw a forest of masts and their hearts fluttered with joy because they thought their troubles were over. They thought they had found there a city and its inhabitants, like in Grippia, but they were far off. The masts, blanched by foul weather, bore no sails.

Then, while the strong current hurled them toward port, a sailor who had climbed to the top of the mast, yelled down to the knights: "Bold knights, prepare yourselves for life eternal! We are not saved, we are going to be trapped in place because the mountain we see stands in the middle of the Congealed Sea.* We shall all perish if God does not save us. Knights, I shall tell you of the strength of this rock and the virtue granted it by nature. It rapidly draws to it all ships sailing within a thirty-mile radius; this is the pure truth. If a ship contains any iron it is useless to steer it, it is compelled to dash itself upon the mountain. There where we see the boats at the foot of this dark rock, there is where we shall die of hunger. There is nothing that can be done; this is what always happens to sailors who risk sailing in these regions."

Duke Ernst then spoke to his knights: "Dear companions in arms, let us now beseech God for His welcome to His kingdom! We are going to perish at the foot of this mountain." The knights weighed the words of the duke and followed his advice.

Once they had said their prayers and made peace with their conscience, the exiles proclaimed their distress to God, imploring the Creator to save their souls. In the meantime, they had drawn so close to the mountainous rock that they could clearly see the ships with their large masts. The magnet attracted their boat so quickly and with such

---

*This is called *Oceanus caligans* in Latin, *mer betée* in Middle French, and *lebermer* in Middle High German. It involves a mythical vision of an icefield.

force that it pushed aside all the other ships. The violence of the shock was so great that the other ships all collided together, their masts swayed and struck one another; some ships were smashed into pieces. Through a miracle, none of the knights were hurt by the worm-eaten masts that struck their boat, which, wonder of wonders, stood firm. The brave knights got a close glimpse of death, but God allowed them to reach the foot of the mountain safe and sound. When the ship came to a halt, the knights did what everyone who is doomed to be stuck somewhere for a long time does: they jumped down off the boat and each went his own way to examine the wreckage that, like a forest, surrounded the mountain. They discovered fabulous amounts of wealth beyond all telling, a wealth of gold, silver, precious stones, purple cloth, velvet, and lustrous silk. The duke and his knights then scaled the mountain to see if they could catch sight of any land. None of them found any means of leaving the island, which vexed them mightily. The mountain stood in the middle of the sea, and the gallant warriors were therefore doomed to die of starvation. They accepted death as atonement for their sins.

Once the foodstuffs they had taken from Grippia were exhausted, they began dying one after another until there only remained the duke and six of his men. A griffin carried off the dead.[8] This is how the survivors behaved: each time one of them succumbed to hunger, they quickly removed the cadaver from the boat and deposited it on the bridge. The griffins would come and take it back to their nest where they fed it to their young. The duke suffered greatly from his inability to stop the slow death of his companions. The survivors withered and shared the half of a loaf of bread remaining to them. Count Wetzel then made this suggestion: "I have just thought of a strategy for getting us out of this situation. If we wish to be saved there is but one solution. We must hunt for hides in the shipwrecked boats and put on our good armor. Once we have sewn ourselves into the hides, we must immediately lie down on the ship's prow and, protected by our armor, the griffins will be able to carry us without wounding us.[9] Once we have seen that they have gone off in search of food, we can remove these skins and descend from their nests. If God does not wish for us to save ourselves, it will be better to die fighting than to meet an end with no glory."

All thought this idea had been inspired by God, and they raced to the boats where, to their great joy, they found many sea-cow hides. They cut one of these hides into strips to be used to sew the other skins together. All was ready within the space of a night, and they then deliberated to determine who would be the first. Count Wetzel said: "My lord and I will be the first. I shall seal us inside two hides because, alive or dead, I do not want to part from him so that we may confront all dangers together. Let fate decide whether we shall be saved or not, we shall share the same destiny. If God wishes us to escape, the griffins will not be long in carrying you away as well, so do not weep. No one can

say how strong these birds are. If all goes well, we shall see something that would occur later." At dawn, the two knights donned their armor, putting on their helmets, shields, leg guards, and they laid their bare swords close by. They were then sewn into the sea-cow hides, and their comrades placed them on the deck while weeping. The duke implored his men to sew each other into the strong hides and entrust themselves to God. Parting company was painful.

As they habitually did, the griffins flew to the boats and, seeing the bundles on the bridge, each seized one in its talons[10] and carried it back to their nest to toss it to their young. The fledglings tried vainly to open them in order to enjoy their contents. The two knights split the hides open and went down into the forest where the griffins could not reach them. They thanked their Creator for saving them and sought refuge beneath the thick foliage. The griffins returned to again carry off two more men to their nest. They, too, freed themselves and made their way down, thus escaping the young griffins. Without any delay, the griffins did this a third time and two other knights sealed within the hides were carried off and freed like the previous ones. The last knight was too weak and died on the ship. When the duke saw them, his heart overflowed with joy. He ran to greet them and embraced them all.

Our heroes decided to travel through the forest, but they found no food and had to eat plants and anything else they deemed edible.

They eventually came to a fast river flowing with clear water. There they were able to catch fish with their hands and cook them over a fire. They then went in search of a crossing point both up- and downstream, but quickly became disillusioned: cliffs looped up on one side, and on the other a high mountain rose into the clouds. The river flowed with an indescribable violence and with a great roar poured into a gorge so mightily that once again the knights believed their last hours were upon them.

"Let us think," said the duke. "If we stay here, we shall die."

"Then, since we cannot cross, we need to try something else!" Count Wetzel replied. "Let us build a raft with no further delay, one that is large and solid enough to carry us. We must travel through this gorge. There is no other possibility. God shall decide our fate: either we make it across or we die."

They all set themselves to work, cutting down trees with their swords, gathering them together and connecting them with solidly woven willow branches, and then they embarked putting their fate in the hands of Our Lord, His mother, and all the saints. The strange adventures of these knights are still told today.

The water carried them into the cavern where the river disappeared. Tossed about in every direction, scared witless, they plunged into the darkness. Suddenly, a light appeared: a magnificent array of multicolored stones cast a bright gleam, making even the depths of the water sparkle. Ernst spied a gem that he tore off the wall when passing. It is

this stone, called an orpheline,* that can be seen on the imperial crown. If you do not believe me, go to Bamberg to consult the master who wrote this story! Moreover, it exists in Latin, therefore it is a true story.

The romance then relates the duke's encounter with the Arimaspians (the Cyclops), the Long Ears (the Panoteans), the Shadow Feet, the Sciapods, the Pygmys, and the giants (ll. 4499–6593). Ernst brought back from his journey several specimens of people from the ends of the earth and, on his return to Bamberg, offered the emperor an Arimaspian, a Panotean, and a Pygmy.

Panotean

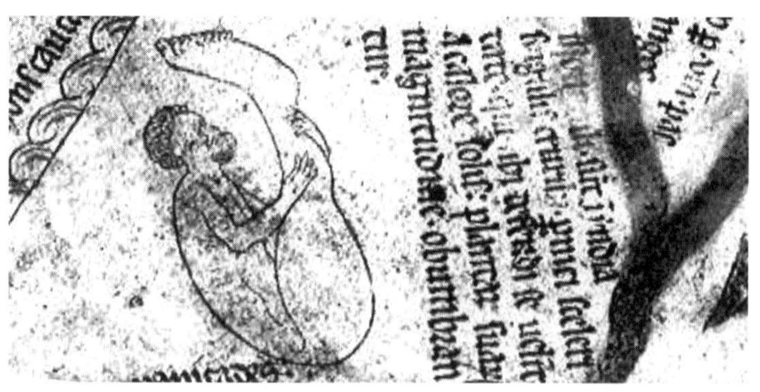

Sciapod

Der waise, "the orphan."

The Jewish traveler Benjamin of Tudela (ca. 1130–1173) *visited Europe and Africa, and journeyed as far as China, recording the adventures in his* Sefer haMasa'ot *(Book of Travels), which was translated into Latin. He was one of the first to tell of "rescue" by griffins, a rescue we find in Duke Ernst. He reports:*

From thence the passage to China is effected in forty days, this country lies eastward and some say that the star Orion predominates in the sea which bounds it, and which is called Sea of Nikpha.* Sometimes so violent a storm rages in this sea, that no mariner can reach his vessel; and whenever the storm throws a ship into the sea, it is impossible to govern it; the crew and the passengers consume their provisions and then die miserably. Many vessels have been lost in this way, but people have learned how to save themselves from this fate by the following contrivance: They take bullocks' hides along with them and whenever this storm arises and throws them into the Sea of Nikpha, they sew themselves up in the hides, taking care to have a knife in their hand, and being secured against the water, they throw themselves into the ocean; here they are soon perceived by a large eagle called [a] griffin, which takes them for cattle, darts down, takes them in his grip and carries them upon dry land, where he deposits his burden on a hill or in a dale, there to to consume his prey. The man, however, now avails himself of his knife therewith to kill the bird, creeps forth from the hide and tries to reach an inhabited country. Many people have been saved by this stratagem.[11]

German texts: Bartsch, ed., *Herzog Ernst*; Flood, ed., *Die Historie von Herzog Ernst*; King, ed., *Das Lied von Herzog Ernst.*

Latin texts: Ehlen, ed., *Hystoria ducis Bauarie Ernesti*; Gansweidt, ed., *Der "Ernestus" des Odo von Magdeburg*; Jacobsen and Orth, eds., *Gesta Ernesti Ducis.*

*Ning-po?

The illustrations of the Thiebolt Berger edition
(Strasbourg, ca. 1560)

five

Solomon and Marcolf

(*Middle High German*)

This romance first appeared toward the end of the twelfth century, but there are manuscripts dating from the last third of the fifteenth century that still continued to recount the adventures of Marcolf. This latter figure, at the behest of Solomon, headed off into the East to bring the king back his fickle wife. The story is characterized by the use of magic, ruses, and disguise, along with the occasional comic scenes intended to amuse the public.

The book was printed in Strasbourg in 1499 by Mathis Hüpfuff (Matthias Hupfuff) and in 1510 by Johannes Knoblauch. From 1482 onward, it was quite a popular book.

A child was born in Jerusalem who would rule over all of Christendom: this was the wise king Solomon. He married the daughter of a heathen* in India named Cyprian. He abducted her[1] without the consent of her father and forced her to travel over the sea to Jerusalem. Many heroes lost their lives because of her. He had her baptized and taught her the

*[In medieval German literature, the term "heathen" (i.e., pagan) is used generically to refer to any non-Christian. —*Ed.*]

Christian religion, which took a year, and also taught her chess. He always loved her despite what she later put him through.

She was the most beautiful of women: her neck was white as snow, her mouth shone like a ruby, and her sparkling eyes revealed her noble lineage; she had golden and silky hair. She was a woman of enthralling beauty and tremendous charm, with the name of Salome. She wore a tunic of fine silk, a cloak studded with sparkling precious stones, and the band she wore over her forehead was made of gold. A carbuncle radiant like the sun was set in the center of her crown, and her face shone like the morning star.

On the day of Pentecost, the queen went to church accompanied by two powerful princes. Their procession was preceded by minstrels, and to her right were the proud knights who served as her bodyguards, to her left were beautiful maidens. Four groups of vassals clad in splendid garments followed her. When she entered the church, the Mass began. She was handed a psalter written in letters of gold, and when the Gospel was recited, look at the offering she made: a gold ring covered with tiny precious stones. After the sermon, King Solomon and his ravishing wife took a seat at the table. The knights facing them across the table gazed at the queen in fascination, even forgetting to eat and drink. When she brought her golden cup to her lips, the pink of her cheeks was reflected in the wine so strongly it brought her husband Solomon to the peak of bliss. We are told that he loved her, and his greatest happiness was to lie in her snow-white arms when they were in their chamber. But the queen was soon to cause much grief and torment, and she brought about the death of many knights.

Four years passed in this fashion. A powerful heathen prince of the Middle East happened to become infatuated with Salome. His father was the arrogant King Memerolt, and his name was Fore. He ruled with absolute power over the land and its inhabitants. He had thirty-six dukes, fifty counts, and sixteen kings as his vassals. One fine Sunday he called them all together. "I await your counsel," he told them. "I wish to wed a woman of my rank who will rule over the Wendelsee at the edge of the ocean." No one could give him the answer he was seeking. Vexed, Fore lowered his head, and an elder, white with age, took the floor: "I know that on the other side of the sea there is a Christian queen in Jerusalem, the wife of King Solomon. She is beautiful and completely charming. She would be worthy of you."

"I shall abduct her," said Fore enthusiastically, raising his head back up. "Solomon cannot keep her! I am going to leave for Jerusalem with a powerful army and anyone who helps me shall find their fortunes made."

"Sire, she is my daughter," said King Cyprian. "Solomon abducted her and I have never accepted it. I am going to give you four thousand brave men. That she wed a Christian causes me great grief."

The king of Duscan promised five thousand brave warriors:

"I am going to send them to Jerusalem because the idea that she is spending her life among the Christians is a great affliction to me."

"Sire," said King Princian, "I am going to give you six thousand brave men. Thirty-six dukes are in my service and, this is no lie, fifty counts. I will put at your disposal an entire army of thirty thousand men that I am sending to Jerusalem. With so many forces, Solomon will not be able to guard his wife."

An emissary was immediately sent to him. He announced that war was declared to win back Queen Salome. "I am fully capable of preventing this," Solomon replied. "If this proud ruler dares come here, that will be the last thing he ever does!"

Fore had forty vessels filled with a year's worth of food and clothing, and ten days later had sailed within sight of Jerusalem. He told his vassals: "This is the very day that Solomon will be forced to hand over his beautiful wife to me!" But he forgot that this king also had proud knights at his disposal to help him defend his honor.

On entering the port, the sailors made landfall, and the heathen warriors prepared themselves for battle. They set up camp in front of the city. Solomon was therefore under siege by a powerful army. Fore told his standard-bearer, Duke Elian: "We need a messenger who will accept the task of delivering this ultimatum to King Solomon: either he surrenders his beautiful wife to me, or else he must fight me."

"I will take on this responsibility at the risk of my life," said Elian, as he put on an ermine cloak embroidered with gold and made his way to the castle.

At the time King Solomon was sitting in his palace in the company

of Salome and Marcolf, his beloved brother. All three courteously welcomed Elian. Elian knelt before them and delivered his message, but Solomon refused to hand over his wife. "I'd rather give up my life!" he answered.

As Elian was preparing to leave, Marcolf asked him a question: "What is the size of your army?"

"Around forty thousand men."

"Then tell your lord that we will be ready to fight in fourteen days."

Elian returned to Fore and gave him this warning: "Before we can abduct the queen, many proud knights will die."

Solomon sent messengers throughout the land to raise an army of his vassals. The king of Marrach (Morocco) came to Jerusalem with many knights, the burghers of Naples and Marseilles, as well as the powerful sovereign of Sardinia—thirty-five thousand men in all. "Even if the heathens have five thousand more men than us," said the wily Marcolf,* "Christ will not forget us." He had a standard woven from red and gold silk and bearing the figure of Christ, and he carried it personally. The call to battle was sounded, noble kings fell, proud

*The description of Marcolf used here, *"der listige man,"* also means "the clever or cunning man."

knights howled with pain, and the clash of arms noisily resounded. The battle lasted for five days; thirty-five thousand heathens found their deaths, and those who survived, perished at sea. Fore was defeated and captured; Solomon had him brought to his castle where he was given a courteous welcome by Salome. Solomon then asked his people: "What fate should I reserve for him?"

"Sire, think of his main intent for coming here," said the shrewd Marcolf: "He wanted to steal your wife; he should die! If you do not wish to be bothered with this, entrust him to me and I swear you will never hear another word about it." However, Solomon thought this was unworthy of him. "I am going to have him chained in the depths of the dungeon where he can rot," he said, "and Salome will be his warder."

"That does not seem very sensible to me," Marcolf replied. "When the straw is too close to the fire, it will easily catch flame. This is what will happen if you leave Fore in close proximity to your wife."

"What has she done, Marcolf?" Solomon asked him. "Why such distrust? I have no worries, let me assure you."

"If she deceives you, the fault will be yours alone!" Marcolf burst out.

Solomon then lost his temper: "You will fall from my graces forever by doubting the queen's virtue!"

"Sire, by taking this action, you will be forging your own misfortune! You must not come complain to me later," Marcolf shouted back.

Solomon dismissed his advice: he entrusted Fore to be guarded by Salome. Fatal decision! She became his mistress, which is what happens when you leave the nanny goat close to the billy. The cunning Fore seduced the lady with magic; he had a nephew named Elias, a master magician, who enchanted the stone on a ring and sent it to him. Fore offered it to the queen, saying: "Please deign to wear this ring of gold!" She sought out Marcolf and asked him to look at the ring in sunlight to see if she was risking any damage to her honor. Marcolf performed this task, but the gold of the ring gleamed so strongly that he was not able to detect the spell in the stone despite all his knowledge.[2] Salome placed the ring on her finger and she immediately succumbed body and soul, and for all time, to Fore's charm.

One day when he was sitting near her, he said to her: "Do me a favor, noble queen! You realize that I have lost many of my men on account of you."

"How can I do this?" said the queen. "Solomon is a shrewd man, and I fear Marcolf even more."

"If you agree, I am going to dupe both of them. You know full well that they should never have let you come near me. If you see this as a testament of their great wisdom, I swear to you that I am three times smarter than both of them together!"

"Do not overestimate yourself! Nobody has even a tenth of Marcolf's cunning. If I had any hidden intentions, I am sure Marcolf would read them immediately on my face. I am convinced, Fore, that we would be risking our lives."

"I have many powerful vassals, dukes, counts, and kings, and you shall be their queen. I will also free your father Cyprian of his obligations as a vassal to me. Let us leave together, and far from here you shall rule over Wendelsee!"

"I am going to follow you," the queen promised, which filled the evil heathen's heart with joy.

"In six months, I will send a minstrel with two turtle doves," Fore replied; "give him a warm welcome! He will be holding a German harp adorned with gemstones. This is how you will recognize him. He will bring you a magic plant,[3] which, when you eat it in secret, will make you sick. You will fall down upon the grass as if dead, but your skin will keep its beautiful hue. Remove my chains, noble lady!"

She did what he requested and said: "Make sure you leave this land with all speed and send me your messenger on the appointed day, because I no longer wish to be Solomon's wife."

When it was learned at court that the heathen had escaped and fled, the perspicacious Marcolf immediately said: "It is the queen, that traitor, who allowed him to leave!"

"She is innocent," Solomon retorted, "it was a maiden who freed him with no ulterior motive."

"Sire, keep close watch over your wife because, in less than a year, she will have left you! Mighty King Solomon, know that I am going to let things run their course, simply so I can convince you of the truth of what I tell you."

Six months later, Fore's messenger arrived with two turtledoves and a harp. Salome met him while on her way to Mass, and he gave her the magic plant while handing her his harp. She then gave him back his instrument, saying: "Leave the court as quick as you can, before Marcolf takes note of you!" Once she entered the cathedral, the Mass began, but the queen paid no attention to her devotions and had trouble waiting for the final blessing, because all her thoughts were turned to the magic plant. At the end of the service she ingested it in private and immediately collapsed upon the grass as if dead, although her face retained its living hue. When Marcolf heard the news, he said: "There is magic at work here! I encountered the queen this morning and from what I could see she was perky and gay." Solomon went into despair and began tearing out his hair.

"It is a shame to see a prince behave this way!" Marcolf burst out, "A spell has given your wife the rigidity of death. I have some knowledge in medicine; I may be able to help her if I am allowed to examine her."

"Stop, Marcolf! You have already done enough damage to the queen and me—at least spare me your jokes."

Marcolf then thought to himself: "I should really dig into the matter. If it is truly a case of magic and she is not dead, and later she flees, I should set off in pursuit of her to bring her back." So let us see what he did: he took Salome's hand, into which he poured molten gold, but the spell was so strong that she felt nothing,[4] although the molten gold ate into her hand.

"Get out of my sight!" Solomon ordered in a fury, "What do you suspect my wife of doing?"

"I have done what needed to be done because she does not seem to be dead. Your wife's color is as fresh as a rose. I assure you that her death is pure illusion."

Solomon did not believe him and chased him out of his court: "May I never see you again!" Marcolf left.

Seeing a bread oven on his path, he slipped inside of it to mock the king. When Solomon caught sight of his buttocks in the oven, he was beside himself with rage and screamed: "You have never insulted me like this before!"

"You have forbidden me from ever facing you again—well then, have a good look at my backside!" Marcolf responded.

Despite how furious he was, the king could not help himself from laughing. "If your insult had truly affected me, you would have paid for it with your life, and if you were truly my brother, you would not mock me at all and you would not have it in you to laugh, but it is obvious that you are not my brother." Solomon had the queen placed in a casket made of red gold. "That is unfortunate, all that gold wasted!" said Marcolf. "If it was up to me, I would toss her into a swamp,"* and he secretly went to pile stones on top of the casket

*A common punishment for criminals in the Germanic regions.

lid. Three days later, the minstrel opened the casket and fled with the queen by sea.

After five days, motivated by doubt, Solomon went secretly to verify if his wife was still in her casket. When he discovered it broken apart, I imagine he felt a pain like no other; he had been rewarded well for his fidelity! "Oh woe! I dare not announce this news in court in Marcolf's presence," he thought. He then spotted a maiden and bid her come to him. He asked her: "Why did you forget to burn incense over my wife's casket?" He then left. She took a silver incense burner but, on seeing the open casket, rushed to share the news with the court and the king, who pretended he was just learning about it. "The queen has fled. By my faith, my brother predicted this!" he exclaimed. He immediately went in search of Marcolf and told him: "My dear brother, I have come to confirm my distress: the queen has fled."

"Sire," the other answered, "I do not believe your wife has deceived you; she was bewitched by a plant. Even if I were as intelligent as you, as handsome as Absalom, and even if I could sing as well as Horant,* I would not be able to take your wife, except through lies and trickery."

"Lets break this spell!" said the king. "Marcolf, my dear brother, bring the noble queen back to us and I will share rulership over the powerful kingdom of Jerusalem with you. Be my messenger and set off in pursuit of the beautiful fugitive. God will reward you!"

"Mighty king," responded Marcolf, "even if you no longer consider me to be your brother, your wishes are my commands."

He went to the home of an old Jew named Berman, who had a long beard that was white as snow and hung down to his belt. "Advise me," Marcolf said to him. "The king wants to send me in search of his wife." The Jew took him by the hand and led him into a chamber. Then Marcolf took a long knife and stabbed him, then he flayed the skin off the top half of the body, smeared the skin with a balm, and put it on before going to find the king.[5]

*A minstrel from the Middle High German epic *Kudrun;* he was famous for his songs.

"Noble sire, for the love of all women, give me money!"

"Owing to the few joys they bring me, I cannot give you very much," Solomon responded, while giving him three gold marks.

Marcolf then spotted a ring on the king's finger. "Sire, can you give me that ring you are wearing?" The king took it off and handed it to him. Marcolf slipped the ring onto his finger, and bowed courteously, then quickly took his leave, happy that the king had not recognized him.

The shrewd Marcolf went back to his room, took off the skin, put on scarlet garments, and presented himself before Solomon.

"For the love of all women, where is your gold ring?"

"I gave it to a white-bearded old man," the sovereign responded. Marcolf burst out laughing: "Look, I have it on my finger."

Exulting, Solomon embraced him: "Marcolf, you truly perform wonders, even if no one knows what you are up to." The king had a pilgrim's staff and an attractively decorated knapsack brought to his brother. Marcolf said his farewells to him. "If I do not find the queen, I will spend the rest of my life wandering as a pilgrim through the world. Sire, I entrust you with my little boy Malen." The child was summoned forth and Solomon told him: "I hereby grant you all the fiefs of your father."

Then Marcolf took to the sea in a leather skiff that was sealed tight with pitch and was equipped with two openings. He also knew how to steer it! Even a storm would not be able to capsize it. He sailed for seven long years before reaching Wendelsee and guided his skiff through the reeds until he reached the bank, where he abandoned his craft. On the path he saw an old heathen passing by and cried out to him: "You are going to die!" But the man begged him to spare him, adding: "I have long been a porter at the castle of Wendelsee."

"What's new at the castle?" Marcolf asked. "It is said that your lord has a very beautiful wife that he loves with a burning love, more than his own life."

"She shines like a rose; I have never seen such a beautiful sovereign," the other replied.

Marcolf then pulled out his long and richly decorated sharp knife and stabbed the heathen in the heart with it. He threw the corpse into a deep ditch while telling it: "If anyone questions you, you will not be able to reveal anything." Then he quickly slipped into the skin of the Jew Berman, put on a heavy woolen coat, attached an olive branch to the collar, picked up a crutch that he put under his armpit, and it was in this disguise that he made his way to the palace, where he found King Fore and his men practicing chivalrous games, throwing the javelin or the stone.

In the middle of the courtyard, the story tells us, stood a large linden tree. Beneath it was a bench reserved for nobility; any commoner who sat there was condemned to death. This was where Marcolf sat himself down though and stuck his crutch in the grass. A bell hung in the courtyard; when it rang, Fore and his knights made their way to the service. Marcolf remained seated, though he was firmly asked to vacate the premises. He refused to back off, not even a step. A chamberlain* came with five servants armed with staffs, but he threatened him: "No, brave warrior, if you hit me even a single time, I will strike you in return with my crutch so hard that you will think of me until the Day of the Last Judgment!" which made Fore laugh. "Let this stranger rest here,"

*Throughout the text this term (*kemerer*) is used with the meaning of "official."

he said. "I see by his behavior that he is of noble birth!" and he went on his way to church, followed by the beautiful Salome. When she passed before him, Marcolf recognized her and was delighted to be at the end of his quest. He leaped to his feet and courteously bowed before her.

The service went on for a long time, and Marcolf cursed the heathen priest: "Damned Saracen, what are you singing on about today? May a thousand devils carry you away!" When everyone came out of the church, Marcolf stood up and stood in the queen's way. When passing by him, she asked him: "What do you want, pilgrim? Where do you come from, old man?"

"Noble queen, trusting in your charity, I have made a long voyage by sea and have come here to ask you a favor . . ."

"If you stay here, I shall give you bread and wine."

"I am a sinner and can stay nowhere for very long. I would like to remain here for two weeks; can you ensure that I lack for nothing during this time?" asked Marcolf.

"Did you travel by way of Jerusalem?" the queen asked. "Did you see King Solomon and his brave vassal, Marcolf?"

"I went through Jerusalem seven years ago and I found them in deep sorrow. The queen had died suddenly and they had buried her beneath a large stone, which did not prevent the devil from carrying her off to hell."

Salome turned away to laugh, then she took him by the hand and ordered her chamberlain: "Ensure that the night is gentle to this exhausted pilgrim and make sure that he does not lack for wine!"

Marcolf was wearing a breastplate beneath his clothing. A young duchess had caught a glimpse of it and went to see Salome after the meal to tell her.

"Milady, if you permit me, I would like to talk to you about that pilgrim. I saw that he is wearing a breastplate of good steel; he is surely a bold knight."

"Have him come to me immediately," responded the fair lady. "Since he has journeyed here from across the sea, perhaps he will reveal the reason for his coming to me."

The duchess set off in search of Marcolf and found him in the courtyard. "Hail, stranger, you must go join the queen at once! You must go now and tell her all the latest news; milady loves to listen to this and cannot stand waiting."

"Charming maiden, let me rest until the morning. If she wants news, I will give her a wealth of it tomorrow."

"You must come with me at once," the young woman insisted.

Fearing for his life and dreading the bloodthirsty queen, Marcolf turned a deaf ear to her entreaties.

Fore left to go hunting the next day, and, after reflecting on the matter, Marcolf went to find the queen to entreat her to play a game of chess with him. "I need money," he said; "I'll wager my head in this match against gold!" Hoping to pull off a stunning victory, she had a chessboard brought in. It was inlaid with gold and precious stones such as emeralds and white, red, yellow, and green hyacinths.

"Go ahead, stranger, but you do not have the ghost of a chance and I am going to take your head."

"What will you wager?" Marcolf asked.

"Thirty gold marks and a safe conduct to let you go wherever you would in our land!" Salome answered.

"I would rather you made your most beautiful servant the stakes."

"Do you know how to handle yourself with the maidens?" the queen asked, bursting out in laughter.

"If I win, she will be my companion."

"All right, then choose one."

He pointed to the sister of King Fore, who began to laugh: "Fore is my brother. Even if you win, you will lose."

"If you refuse, then I decline to play."

He had barely finished speaking when the maiden sat next to him in front of the chessboard. "Begin, foreign pilgrim; I think I can protect you against the duplicity of the queen. Begin brave hero; you are safe here from the sovereign's maneuvers. I think you are a quite capable man. If you win, I accept risking adventure with you."

The queen began playing, but Marcolf, who was on his guard, countered her skillfully while leaving her the initiative.

"I have never met my master at chess,"[6] she said. "Your haughtiness will be your undoing."

"I have traveled in many lands, and yet I have never been beaten."

Marcolf moved a piece and attacked the king. "I can assure you that your head is already wobbling on your shoulders," said Salome. "I will have it cleanly lopped off. You made your play too quickly! With my knight, I put you in check and mate." Our pilgrim let out a great fart.

"What have you done there, old pilgrim?" laughed the queen.

"You repeated I was going to lose my head so many times that I grew scared," he responded. "If you win the match, then I lose my life." But he did not really believe this.

He implored Salome to sit down next to him. He recognized the place where he had pierced her hand with the liquid gold because the sun passed through her glove. He was therefore certain that she was Solomon's wife.

He had brought a gold ring on which a nightingale had been skillfully attached; he slipped on the ring and immediately the bird opened its beak and began to sing in a melodious voice.[7] Fascinated, she stared at it, while Marcolf took her knight and two other pawns. This was how he got himself out of the bind and won the match. "Do you give up, queen? Has the pilgrim saved his head?" He began singing gaily, to Salome's great dismay. He was a peerless singer who enthused all who heard him. He sang an ancient melody of King David,* which was particularly sweet to the ear. The queen asked him: "Where did you learn these songs that I often heard at my father's table?"

"Once upon a time I was minstrel who went by the name of Stolzelin;† I sang in return for a good reward. But out of love for God I abandoned this life to become a pilgrim. Noble lady, I long wandered through mountains and vales, then I came to Gilest, the city where lives the sun, near a country called India, and that is where I learned

*In the Bible, David sings before Saul.

†"Little Proud One."

this song. I then heard it again in Jerusalem, in King Solomon's palace. There it was sung by Marcolf, a duke of proud bearing."

"Be quiet! You are Marcolf, the vassal of Solomon! Once Fore returns, we will put an end to you."

"You are mistaken. The last time I saw Marcolf he was a beardless young man; look at my gray hair!"

"You are Marcolf, the one who put a hole through my hand with molten gold, and which has caused me such terrible pains. I swear to you that you will never see Jerusalem again!"

Marcolf then stripped off the skin of the Jew Berman, thereby revealing his beautiful blond curls.

"It is certainly me," he told her. "And before I lose my life, many unpleasant things will happen to you. I have followed a long road in order to find you; grant me at least a truce until the morning's light, I ask nothing else."

"Silence! You are so wily that you could not even be held captive behind a thousand locks!"

Marcolf threw himself down on the ground before the queen, imploring her insistently to grant him his request, and he did not cease until she granted him a truce.

When evening came, he went to find Salome and told her: "Majesty, command one of your servants to accompany me on a stroll by the edge of the sea. One who shall not see noon the next day wishes to distract himself as best as he is able." An old Saracen broke in: "Noble queen, you should not refuse him." Salome accompanied Marcolf personally and, out of precaution, added an escort of sixty warriors. Once they reached the shore, they gazed at the horizon.

"Wouldn't you like to come with me to Jerusalem?" Marcolf asked the queen.

"Shut your mouth! You hurt me enough already when I lived in that city. Tomorrow, before the sun sets, you will be swinging from a branch, I swear!"

"Then may God have pity on my soul! Let me go closer to the water though, for I wish to confess my sins to the reeds; you know there is no other confessor in these parts."

"Your ruse will not work," she responded, and then she put him in the hands of twelve heathens. "Guard this sly fox well. If he escapes, you will pay for it with your lives."

The queen returned to the palace with Marcolf. She went to bed and he remained alone with his guards, to whom he told stories until they were exhausted and falling asleep. He then coughed in such a way that it blew the candle out. One of the heathens asked: "Why did you do that?"

"It was an accident. Bring another candle and we can continue to amuse ourselves. Place two sentinels in front of the door; you will have no fear that I might escape."

Marcolf had a plan. He took from a hiding place a little flask of a numbing drink, which he poured into a nearby gold cup. "You gentlemen must be thirsty," he said. "This wine comes from Cypress; it was given to me by the queen. Daybreak is upon us; drink it all as I no longer need it. As you know, your liege lord has refused to grant me grace! And you may keep the cup." All of them sank into slumber except for one who, cup in hand, thoughtfully contemplated his companions.

"Why are you sleeping now?" he asked them with surprise. "If this Christian escapes us, our lives will not be worth a whit."

"So drink!" Marcolf said, "Because you are the last one to drink, the cup will belong to you."

The heathen drank, the cup fell from his hands, and he collapsed on the ground like the others. His calm restored, Marcolf regained his courage. He took some scissors from his backpack and cut the heathens' hair above their ears, then, with a razor, quickly gave each of them a tonsure. He then made his way to the door and asked the porter to let him out.

"The queen ordered me to go catch some fish for her immediately."

"I dare not let you leave before daybreak," the guard answered, "it is the queen herself who forbid me to let you out."

Marcolf entered the guardroom and said: "Porter, my friend, open the door for me and this evening I will read your future in the stars."

"All right, I will open the door for you."

The porter approached the gate with the key, but Marcolf heaved a stone up and killed him. The guard's wife came running out, ready to shout "Murder!" but Marcolf, according to the story, slew her with a stone as well. Grabbing the key, he raced to his skiff, set sail upon the open sea, and kept sailing until dawn.

When she awoke, the queen learned that her guards had been given tonsures and were plunged into a deep sleep, and that Marcolf had fled by sea.[8] She climbed onto the ramparts; when she spotted the fugitive, she wept hot tears and fell to the ground in despair. "Did I not give you sufficient warning? If you bring him back to me, I will give you thirty gold marks," she told her men. Duke Marsilian boarded a galley with fifty men and set off in pursuit of Marcolf. He saw them approaching and, while they drew up alongside his boat, he hid a silver flask beneath his belt. He then fled while cursing: "The devil must have carried off all the reeds that should have been here!" Unable to hide, he was captured and his hands were bound so tightly that blood squeezed out from under his nails. While the heathens set up on the bank, two knights left to alert the queen. As a reward, she gave them a valuable cloak with bright colors.

As night fell, twelve men kept guard over Marcolf, who remained tied and bound. Look at what he said: "If you unbind me, I will tell you many tales of what I've known among the Jews and heathens, for I have traveled far and wide." Four men untied him and he began telling stories of his adventures until he complained that he was thirsty. He took the flask out and brought it to his mouth as if he intended to take a drink from it. This was when the heathens were introduced to his cunning ways: he did not drink a single drop and told them: "Gentlemen, if you are thirsty, drink! You have never tasted a better wine." He handed them the flask, and they drank so much that they were soon rolling on the ground.[9] As for the one who had bound him so cruelly, he decapitated him with his own sword. "Here is your just reward! I need your clothes to appear before the queen." Marcolf dragged the other eleven so roughly by their hair to toss them into the water that they were bald by the time they got there. "There you are now, with proper tonsures!" he said. "Now you can all sing Mass together, as a manifold voice in the cathedral choir. Even a bishop could not pull off that feat!" He went back to his skiff and took to the sea back to the castle of Wendelsee.

He disembarked, raced to the castle gate, and said: "I have crossed the sea. Marcolf has been captured, and I have come to announce it to the queen!" He was allowed in. Clad in his stolen clothing and with his blonde curls, he could readily be mistaken for a chamberlain. Fore and his court were easily fooled.

"Give us your news!" the king commanded.

"Sire, we have captured him; he can never escape again."

"Then I shall be able to rest easy!"

The bogus chamberlain prepared his bed, which was blessed by twelve clerics,* and Fore went to sleep there in the company of Salome—and Marcolf sprang into action! Without being recognized, he knelt down and gave them a numbing potion that put them into a deep slumber. When the clerics sought to leave the chamber, Marcolf gave them the potion and they all became unconscious. He piled them all together at the foot of a wall, then pulled Fore out of the bed and placed him next to a young cleric. He took the robe off of the oldest cleric and easily slipped it onto the king. He then took the naked man and placed him in the royal bed stretched out alongside the queen. To finish, he took out his scissors and cut Fore's hair to above his ears, then he grabbed a razor and gave him a tonsure, saying: "There you go, now you are the first of the bishops!" Marcolf then went back to sea.

When Fore woke up, he thought he would stay in bed a little longer, wanting to indulge in love play with the queen, and he stretched out his hand to the young cleric. The young man gave him such a

*The text employs the word *cappelân,* literally meaning "chaplain," sometimes in reference to clerics and sometimes to servants (acolytes).

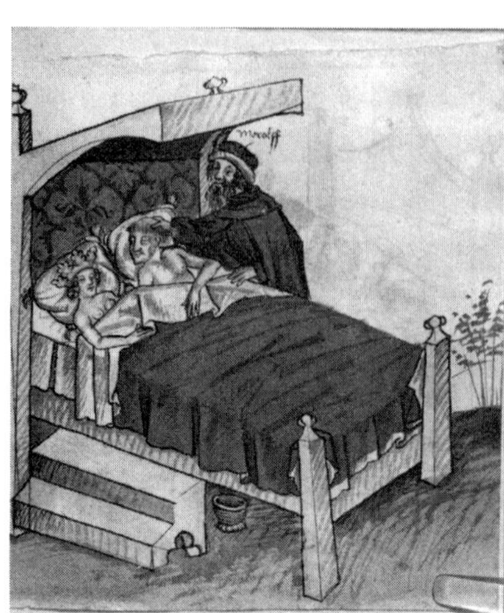

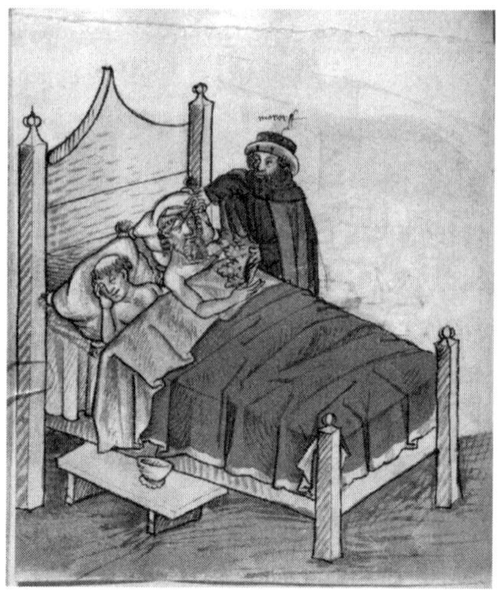

powerful punch to the ear that it left him dazed. When he had regained his senses, Fore said: "Noble queen, for the seven years we have been together, you have never yet behaved like this." Looking down, he saw he was wearing a robe and shouted: "What devil put this on me? This is certainly a new trick of Marcolf's." When he returned to his bed, he found a naked cleric lying there next to Salome. He grabbed him by the legs and pulled him onto the floor while exclaiming: "Get out of here! Hurry off to say morning prayers and leave me with my wife! You have clearly spent a more pleasant night than I did!" The cleric got up and scampered away. Fore approached the bed and patiently waited for Salome to wake up, but she was sleeping so soundly that he eventually said: "You can wake up now, if you please!" When she opened her eyes and saw him, she was angry beyond measure.

"Mighty king, what demon gave you that tonsure?"

"It was the will of God; we must atone for the sin we committed by deceiving Solomon."

A powerful voice echoed through the castle. It was Marcolf, who was singing so loudly at sea that it was causing the entire castle to echo. Fore climbed up to the ramparts and yelled: "Marcolf, stop for a moment so the queen can greet you."

"I cannot tarry," he replied. "Tell me quickly what message I should pass on to my lord! You may be sure that I am going to Jerusalem and that Solomon is going to attack you with a powerful army."

Fore ordered his people to capture the fugitive. In an instant Marcolf found himself encircled by twenty-four galleys, but he dove into the sea in front of all the heathens. A hollow tube permitted him to breathe; he had fashioned it from solid leather and attached it to his skiff so firmly that no one could tear it off. He remained hidden in the depths of the water for two full weeks. Thirty-six days later, driven by the winds, he entered Jerusalem after a seven-year absence.

He caught sight of Solomon surrounded by his vassals, but no one recognized the stranger who had tears in his eyes. When Solomon tried to leave, Marcolf implored him to stay yet a little longer: "King, if you like news I can give you some, for I have traveled the world from the Elbe to Termont, before returning to Jersualem." Solomon took him by the hand and courteously led him to a marble crenel. Marcolf began telling him of his adventures.

"You remind me of Marcolf, my loyal vassal," said the king. "I sent him in search of my wife, but he must have perished in the land of the heathens."

"Sire, that is unfortunately true. We wandered together on a pilgrimage for seven years, and I buried him in heathen soil. He charged me with passing on this news."

Solomon burst out sobbing, then got a grip on his emotions: "Where did you bury him, pilgrim?" he asked. "Tell me the truth! His remains are so dear to me that for nothing in the world would I leave them in a heathen land. Henceforth, I care not about my crown, I care not about my kingdom; nothing matters to me. I can never overcome the pain of losing Marcolf. He was my brother, and it was out of love for me that he undertook this journey. I am going to consecrate myself into the service of God starting today." When Marcolf heard the monarch's despair, he said: "Sire, I am Marcolf, the most faithful of all your servants. I have found your wife and, if you wish to win her back, many knights must risk their lives for good or for ill."

Solomon felt happy and sad at the same time, and he embraced his friendly vassal: "Because I have gotten you back, I leave all sorrow aside!" Marcolf went into a room to disguise himself. He slipped on a coat of mail, whose shining rings were so delicately forged that no one would notice it beneath his clothes. He put on a helmet and over it a gray felt hat. He then draped a coarse woolen cloak over himself, stuck an olive branch by his collar, and went in search of Solomon. A valet immediately leaped up and punched him, shouting: "This is for you, wretched beggar man! How dare you come before the king wearing these miserable rags?"

"You are wrong," our man replied. "I have never been struck before a mighty prince. If killing you was not a sin, you would pay for this with your life," and he smote him with such a punch that it left his victim stretched out cold at the feet of the king. The royal guards leaped to their feet, but Marcolf retreated to the door, shouting: "This crutch accompanied me three times over the sea. Anyone I bless with it shall remember it for the rest of his life!" Solomon stood up, called back his guards, and then approached the beggar. Peering under his hat, he recognized Marcolf.

"It is Marcolf," said the king. "He wanted to show us the full range of his ruses and is going to explain to us how we can take back my wife."

"That is exactly what I am going to do!"

Marcolf took off his coat of mail and gave it to the valet, who had to carry it. "May the devil take you!" the servant said. "It was not worth the pain of striking me." Solomon stepped in: "Marcolf, tell us what actions we should take!"

"Sire, organize a tournament. It will draw together a number of heroes. Choose an army of ten thousand men from among them and wherever you carry our standard, none will be able to resist us."

Solomon organized the tournament and introduced Marcolf to the other lords, who gave him a warm welcome and offered to help in winning back the queen. He chose ten thousand men and told Solomon: "Listen to me. Open your chests and distribute your gold to the heroes. This way they will stick with me through all ordeals, wherever I go." The king had all his treasures and precious stones brought forth, of which each man received a portion.

The boats were ready on the shore, Marcolf set sail with the king and ten thousand men, and he set a course for Wendelsee. He said to Solomon:

"I have been assured that you possess great wisdom, and it could never be more useful than it is today."

"When we were in Jerusalem, I obeyed you and I shall continue to heed your counsel," the king replied.

On their arrival in the land of the heathens, Marcolf grabbed the standard and led the army on a narrow path through a dark forest where he allowed the road-weary men to rest.

"We are close to the castle," he told Solomon. "You must venture your life and capture it, if you wish to see your wife again. Yes, she is certainly beautiful and attractive, but she is sharing her bed with a heathen. Doesn't that irritate you at all?"

"Marcolf, what did I do to you for you to force me to put my life at risk? Have I earned your wrath in some way?"

"Sire, it cannot be any other way. You love Salome too much, and you cannot compel her to return except at peril of your life."

"I no longer love her! She has fallen for a heathen, and if I had known this in Jerusalem, I would never have set sail."

"You can leave without any fear; I can easily protect you. If you are recognized by anyone, take this crutch and show yourself as a fighter!"

The king put on a coat of mail that his clothes kept hidden, then Marcolf gave him a good sword and a cap, beneath which was attached a steel helmet. To complete the outfit, he attached a small horn to the collar of his pilgrim's robe.[10] "If you sound this horn," said Marcolf, "I will come to your aid with the ten thousand men."[11] He led the king out of the forest and they soon saw the splendid castle of Wendelsee.

"This is where Fore lives with a large number of heathens."

"Come with me closer to the castle," Solomon commanded.

"Have you lost all spirit?" Marcolf responded angrily. "I was already in that fortress and had all the trouble in the world escaping from it."

The king moved away, saying: "If I am meant to die there, I commend my soul to your care."

"Sire, nothing is going to happen to you. Your fate is in your own hands; we will end up having Fore at our mercy and we shall kill him. But if your good looks betray you, admit your identity and make sure you are judged before the dark forest; I will race to your rescue with ten thousand men and we will wipe out the heathens!"

Marcolf went back into the forest, and Solomon, lost in dark

thoughts, made his way to the castle where Fore's sister gave him a friendly reception. She bade him welcome and asked him: "Where do you come from? Your face is so handsome that if you wished to remain near me, you would lack for nothing until we are parted by death."

"I am a great sinner and cannot remain long at any one place. This is the punishment that has been inflicted on me, and I must wander the world as a pilgrim until my dying day."

"Pilgrim, instead of mortifying yourself, you would be better off giving happiness to a woman."

The maiden rushed to find Salome.

"Alas, my dear queen, a very handsome pilgrim has just arrived at court, the most handsome man ever won by a woman. He has the eyes of a wild falcon—it could well be the king of Jersualem who has come here for you. His brow is distinguished and his eyes shine with a unique gleam."

"Woe to you, Marcolf!" Salome exclaimed. "If you sent him here, you can be sure you shall never see him again alive."

"No harm should be done to him because he was recognized! I am going to tell him to leave immediately if he values his life."

Seeing that Fore's sister was upset, she soothed her this way: "Tell him to stay. I want to see him with my own eyes." She signaled four valets. "Bring the stranger here at once!" she ordered. Once he was present, she greeted him: "Welcome Solomon, my husband! Believe me, I deeply regret that Marcolf escaped and we were unable to capture him so that we could hang him high with a short rope."

"You reveal thus your perfidy! As for Marcolf, he went on behalf of my honor. I am telling you: either you return with me or else Marcolf will kill you!"

"I renounce your love; King Fore is three times more dear to me than you ever were, and I want to spend my life with him. I am certain that he will call a tribunal to sit in judgment of you."

"Allowing me to leave safe and sound is the only way you can prevent Marcolf from coming here to kill you."

"You want me to let you leave? Certainly not! You are going to swing from the branch of a tree."

Solomon was led into a chamber where he was hidden behind a curtain. Time seemed to drag on forever to him, until Fore sat down at the table with Salome. Once they were settled, she brought the conversation around to Solomon.

"A very handsome pilgrim just arrived at our court; it could easily be the king of Jerusalem. Tell me what should be done with him."

"Solomon cannot stay here. If it is is truly him and he behaves courteously toward me," said Fore, "I will allow him to leave."

"You are overlooking what he is capable of! Once free, he will try to kill you. He is there, behind the curtain; summon him before you without any delay and take what action you will. I will submit to your will."

Fore's sister leaped to her feet: "If you listen to Salome, what will happen, Brother? She has betrayed her true husband. If you wish to keep your life, give her back to Solomon! It should be enough to have caused him so much harm already that he did not deserve."

"I wish him no harm, but I want to keep the queen with me for the rest of my life."

His sister went in search of a cup of wine and gave it to Solomon, saying: "Drink, noble prince! Your own wife has betrayed you." He drank and gave her back the cup.

"Beautiful maiden, accompany me to Jerusalem—you deserve to be a Christian."

"If I was allowed to go with you, I would do so gladly because you appear to be a gentleman to me. I fear hurting you because they are watching us so closely. Present yourself to my brother and speak courteously, and he will allow you to return home."

"How can I do that when your brother stole my wife? His life belongs to me!"

"Think instead of how you have no one here to protect you. In this situation, it is better to be friendly toward him." Solomon courageously approached Fore and boldly told him: "Fore, you dishonorable man, what grief you have given me by taking my wife! I should kill you."

"You are mocking me," the heathen replied. "May God forgive you those words. You know full well that it is because of your wife that I lost many knights, and that you captured and imprisoned me for three years. Salome freed me, and it is for her that you now risk your life? Alas, King Solomon, why did you cross the sea?"

"Fore, what I did to you was due to the fact that you callously declared war on me because of my queen. I should have killed you then! But you have behaved poorly toward me, and you shall pay for that with your life."

"Mighty king, tell me true, in accordance with your faith, when I was in your hands as you are now in mine, would I have been allowed to leave safe and sound?"

"I should have ordered my men to raise a gallows and hang you from it."

"You have delivered your own judgment. Vassals, keep close watch over him until tomorrow! Erect a sturdy gallows at the edge of the forest and we shall hang the mighty emperor. Once he is dead, the queen shall be mine alone and no longer have any fear of Marcolf's arrival."

Salome then spoke: "Well said, Fore! If you kill him, I swear to remain with you until the end of my days." In a rage, Fore had Solomon put in chains, which dismayed his sister. The beautiful maiden was filled with pity for him because of his imminent death. She went to her brother and said: "Until today, I have never asked anything from you. I beseech you to place this powerful monarch in my care for the night so that he does not have to remain in chains. This sorry sight pains me. May you never place your trust in me again, dear Brother, if I allow him to escape!"

"How are you going to keep watch over him? Marcolf escaped us at dawn. If Solomon does the same, we shall regret it the rest of our lives."

"I give you my head and our common kingdom as pledge. I swear to you that, if I allow him to return to sea, I will never ask anything of you ever again."

"This pledge is sufficient, but if you allow him to escape, I shall have your head for it, even though you are my sister!"

Then, as she was preparing to leave, Fore held her back: "I ask that you treat him well, for he is a famous prince. I would be distressed if any mishap were to befall him. If I could, I would allow him to return to Jerusalem, but Salome is opposed to that."

"Brother, I will remind you of these words."

She was then given the iron chains, which she cast against the wall.

"Courage, King Solomon! I have put my head at stake to guard you until dawn, and I count on you for not making me run any risk."

"Fair maiden, I would rather die than put you in danger."

She took him by the hand and led him into a chamber whose walls were adorned with wondrous inscriptions, so that he could pass the long night enjoyably. The maiden invited a minstrel to come who carried a German harp. She offered him a costly coat, telling him: "You need only serve this mighty emperor for one night; me, I'll keep you company." She sat near Solomon upon a mat and consoled him so well that he eventually forgot all his worries. She then brought him something to drink. He took the harp from the minstrel's hands, set it on his lap, and with great skill began to play the enchanting melody of the angels, thinking of his father, King David, who had invented the harp before ancient Troy.

Captivated by the sound he was making, the young queen drew close to him and whispered: "Mighty king, have you wish to flee? My warriors are tired; I am going to send them away to relax. Believe me, Fore loves me so much he would never hurt a hair on my head."

"Maiden, what is my life worth if I lose my soul? I am going to remain near you, tormented by the thought of what awaits me at dawn."

"Then there is nothing more I can do for you. Tomorrow all the heathens—two thousand or more—will come to demand your head. What pain I feel at being unable to help you. You will be condemned to die; I shall never get over my grief!"

"Dry your tears; they make me sad. If I am able to get out of this fix, I will show you my gratitude, noble queen."

During this exchange, daybreak came and Solomon was then led before the tribunal. Fore's relatives and vassals, perhaps two thousand in all, came into the court and requested that the trial begin. "Gladly," Fore responded. Solomon's condemnation was made in the blink of an eye: he was sentenced to be hung at the edge of the dark forest, where he was taken immediately. Fore's sister rode beside him and dried his sweat using her costly mantle. "You deserve praise," she told him, "because instead of growing pale, you are keeping all your color."

Marcolf had not abandoned Solomon—far from it. He rode by himself to the forest's edge and looked in the direction of the castle. When he saw the retinue approaching, he turned around and went back to his men.

"To your feet, bold warriors!" he shouted to them. "It is time to ride to the aid of Solomon, for he is in great danger. God will reward those who venture their lives in defense of their liege lord. Embolden yourselves, knights! If we return to Jerusalem, you shall be showered with gifts. The sea prevents us from any retreat. Spare no thought for your wives and children, but set your minds fully on this battle."

"We will not retreat an inch," said the most brave among them, "even if we must drown in our own blood!"

Marcolf entrusted a troop of soldiers to each of the two Templars who accompanied them. "If God grants us victory, spare no one!" he said. "Duke Friedrich, lead a troop through the forest and remember:

no pain, no reward! Before attacking, let us see what deviltries they are preparing—we are quite capable of undoing them."

In the meantime, the heathens had reached the foot of the gallows. Solomon addressed Salome: "Queen, allow me to blow my horn three times to warn Saint Michael of the imminent arrival of my soul.* When the angels hear it, they will take my soul and not abandon it to the hands of the devil. You are fully aware, noble lady, that every sovereign must blow his horn three times before dying."† Salome responded angrily: "It is Marcolf who gave you that advice! If we allow him to sound his horn," she told the heathens, "it will be our doom. Let us go look more closely at the forest. Solomon is counting on the help of his warriors." The queen's words prompted the wrath of Fore: "Solomon, blow your horn as many times as you like! Even if your army comes to your rescue, you will still be the first to die." This advice suited Solomon well. He then blew his horn with all his might so that all his men would hear it. He then knelt down to pray and took up his pilgrim's staff. Salome said to him: "King, what good is that crutch going to do you? Are you planning some dirty trick?"

*A reference to the "weighing of souls" (psychostasis).

†An allusion to the death of Roland. But the same situation is also found in *König Rother* (King Rother), written at the end of the twelfth century.

"It has accompanied me since my departure," replied Solomon. "I want to keep it with me."

Marcolf had divided the army into three groups: one was black; one was white as snow; and he led the other division, which was gray. Fore's sister scrutinized the edge of the forest carefully and said: "I see a man whose black cloak covers a breastplate that is white as ermine." She turned toward Solomon and asked him: "Tell me, what does the archangel Michael look like?"

"Maiden, if you see a black troop, those are devils that want to steal my soul; if you see a gray troop, those are the kinsmen of your liege lord, a hellish mob; but if you see a white troop, those are angels who are seeking to protect my soul, even if I have sinned. You are going to witness a battle for my soul!"

"It is more likely your own vassals who came with you from Jerusalem and who will not abandon you when danger threatens. So you should rejoice, great king! Do not leave me alone to face the danger and boldly strike my brother's soldiers. That is my dearest wish!"

"Noble queen, I promise to do so, and now be on your guard against the charge of the knights. And if I have victory, I will bring you to Jerusalem."

Solomon sounded his horn for the second time and countless knights emerged from hiding. When Salome saw them, she broke down sobbing and said: "Look! The wind is causing a banner to flutter and it is carried by the devil's own son, Marcolf! I swear to you that he will kill me if he sees me."

Solomon grabbed his staff and pulled out the excellent sword hidden inside it. The heathens then rushed upon him and a rough battle ensued. Surrounded on all sides, Solomon had already killed five hundred men before any of his vassals could come to his aid, and he was exhausted. When Fore saw this, he attacked him with eleven of his warriors, but Solomon slew them. Then Fore attacked him personally with his sharp sword and gave him such a cut with it that the blood spurted from Solomon's ears and he fell to the ground. If Marcolf had not come immediately to his aid, he would have been done for, but he came at a gallop when he saw Solomon in distress. He leaped to the ground, held out his hand to King Solomon, and told him: "Forward! We must massacre Fore and his men!" Fore threw himself on Marcolf and struck him so hard that he fell to his knees. The king's brother stood right back up and, with sword in hand, said: "Defend yourself, heathen! Before the day ends, I will have you hung for having stolen the queen." Fore tried to flee, but Marcolf pursued him and hit him with such force that he could not help but fall to the ground. "Now you will atone for the harm you caused us; I am going to kill you and hang the faithless Salome alongside you." At these words, the queen hid behind Solomon's back and cried: "For the love of all women, save me! Whatever I have done to you, powerful king, I swear never to do it again, and I will accompany you to Jersualem." Marcolf captured Fore and brought him before Solomon. He pushed Salome away and told her: "Faithless woman! Your last hour has sounded!" He grabbed her with one hand while he was firmly holding Fore with the other, and pulled both of them beneath the sinister gallows.

"Why are you forsaking me, Solomon?" Salome cried out. "Everything is Fore's fault. You should hang him! His spells are responsible for all my misfortunes."

"Have you no shame, most faithless woman of them all!" cursed Fore. "If your life is spared, you will eventually betray Solomon too."

"Solomon," Salome broke in, "I am going to tell you a dream. Last night I dreamed that I was lying in your arms and you had never known such happiness. Two falcons landed upon my hand. The meaning of the dream is clear: it predicts the birth of a glorious son who will succeed you on the throne."

"I interpret that dream another way," Marcolf interrupted. "It symbolizes the long branch of a majestic oak and thus a high gallows, from which both of you will hang."

Solomon began to laugh: "Marcolf, take care of Fore and leave this wonderful woman to me! I will be eternally grateful to you for this. She has promised her eternal fidelity to me and I wish to put her to the test."

"It is certain that she deceived you, and mere speculation that she will be faithful to you," replied Marcolf. "If you bring her back, you can expect even more shameful behavior."

With these words, Marcolf hung Fore and spared Salome. He razed the castle of Wendelsee to the ground and across the land he scorched the earth. The proud knights of Jerusalem therefore carried off a stunning victory. "Find the young queen for me," Solomon commanded. "She was generous in her help to me and I wish to bring her to Jerusalem."

Marcolf rushed out to do so, found the maiden, and told her: "The king of Jerusalem has sent me to find you, noble queen."

"Is my brother still alive?"

"Noble queen, let's not speak of him again. I gave him the gallows as a wedding gift and he is now swinging in the air."

She broke down crying: "Now I am all alone in the world! He should have hung his wife, but he placed her under his protection and is bringing her home. This faithless woman betrayed my brother and has his death on her conscience. Marcolf, it is up to you to cut my brother down from the gallows and bury him in the casket where my father already rests. As thanks, I will show you a chamber where you will find much gold."

"I will grant your request," he answered.

He therefore gave Fore a funeral service worthy of his rank. The maiden then brought him into a secret chamber. When she opened the door, he saw, to his great joy, gold and sparkling gems. "Marcolf," she told him, "give your men a rich payment so that they do not abandon you." He summoned his warriors and showered them with riches.

Once the treasure had been divvied up, a great tournament was started and many a knight declared: "God willing, Marcolf, may you undertake many more campaigns like this one!" They then rested for twelve days. The ships meant to transport them waited on the shore, but a new battle was started because they wished to conquer the glorious castle of Duscan's king, Isold. When Solomon and Isold met face to face with swords in hand, the heathen yelled: "If you are the king of Jersualem, my god will not refuse me his aid! You are going to die! Berzian, my father, was slain before Jerusalem, and you ordered the hanging of my uncle Fore. You will never return to your country. I am ready to risk my life to win your beautiful wife." He gripped his sword in both hands and struck Solomon with rage, but the latter swung his sword and decapitated his foe with one stroke. All the heathens then fled back to Duscan as fast as they could. This was how Solomon carried off a glorious victory, and the Christians returned to their boats in triumph.

Solomon led his wife aboard ship, and Marcolf followed with Fore's sister. They set sail for Jerusalem, but the queen was hardly overjoyed to be leaving the heathen land.

Let us now speak of the baptism of Fore's sister. Marcolf went to tend to the maiden and told her: "Noble queen, for your soul's salvation, you must be baptized."

"I have come here with a heavy heart, because the memory of my beloved brother gives me grief. I will never stop mourning his death. Here the country and its cities and castles are foreign to me."

"Stop mourning! I give you my word that you shall be compensated."

"And how? I am of high birth and I refuse to be baptized. Do not insist!"

"Once Salome is dead, you will rule over the powerful kingdom of Jerusalem because I am going to give you Solomon as your husband."

"Then I will accept baptism. Where must I go?"

Marcolf went in search of Solomon and told him: "Noble king, the young queen is ready to be baptized."

"That's your business."

The maiden was led into the cathedral and clad in a fine silk shirt. The mistress of the royal house had a chair brought in, set the maiden on her lap, and said: "You who are to be baptized are too heavy for me; I cannot hold you over the baptismal font!" Two duchesses were strolling around the baptistery when they saw Solomon and told him: "We have absolutely no need of you here. You are one too many! Who knows what your relations with this maiden were like?" She was baptized with the name of Affer, and then led to the Holy Sepulchre; there she consecrated herself and was taught the Christian religion for seven years.

After the ceremony, Marcolf sought out Solomon: "King, if your wife gets up to her old tricks, you must send somebody else to hunt her down and who will be ready to risk his life. But it will not be me, of that you can be sure! I almost died for you."

"She will not start behaving like that again!" the king replied.

It should be known that Salome remained in Jerusalem until she gave birth to a handsome boy. She fully intended to stay there and remain faithful to Solomon until the end of her life. For seven years, the latter had no cause for worry, but let us now listen to this strange story! Things did not turn out as anticipated.

The news came to Aeve that there was no more beautiful woman in the world than the wife of King Solomon. King Princian said to himself: "I am ready to do whatever it takes to win her. I am going to Jersualem, and I will either succeed in carrying her off, or else I will never be seen here again." He headed out to sea with twelve vessels and on the twelfth day reached Jerusalem. Salome and Solomon were on their way to vespers when they encountered Princian disguised as a pilgrim. After the Mass, Princian made his way to the castle, where he asked the queen for something to drink. She brought him a goblet fashioned from red gold and handed it to him. After he drank, the heathen snuck a ring into the goblet, and when Salome drank from the cup in turn, she was possessed by an irresistible love for Princian. Marcolf had witnessed the whole thing and he told Solomon: "Sire, what I just observed could easily do you great wrong. You should know that these strangers are not real pilgrims; they covet your wife. She is planning to deceive you again."

"Marcolf, of just what are you accusing my irreproachable queen? She truly wishes to remain here forever."

"Sire, think long and hard on this; it is not a sure thing that I will have any desire to help you if you have need of me," replied Marcolf before walking away.

Twelve weeks later, Salome fled with Princian back to the land of the heathens. Marcolf came before Solomon and said: "Sire, now you must personally set off in search of the queen."

"Stop reproaching me," the king said while weeping. "I entrust my kingdom and my subjects to your care. For my part, I am going to do all I can to find my faithless wife."

Seeing Solomon's despair, Marcolf said to him: "Swear to me that if I bring Salome back, you will give me permission to kill her!" The king swore the oath. "I will bring her back wherever she may be. And I will need to use all of my cunning to do so," Marcolf concluded.

He cut his hair and put two rings in his ears and a third—it is hard to believe—in his neck. He endured this suffering because of the queen. He then ate a plant that made him bloat up as if he was ill. This made him unrecognizable. When he showed himself to Solomon (who should have given him the prize for subterfuge!), tears flooded the king's eyes. "Don't leave! If you become sick or if your ship becomes a plaything of the wind, no one will be able to save you." Marcolf yanked open his slavin,* "Sire, look at how much I have been transformed! I did it for you. Prove your friendship to me by taking care of Fore's sister. If I should not return, marry her!"

Marcolf summoned a doctor, who tied his feet to his thighs in such a way that he left Jersualem looking like he was a legless cripple;[12] furthermore, he pretended to be cross-eyed. He made his way to the shore riding a donkey where he set sail on his skiff, accompanied by the animal. He sailed thirty-six days before the winds brought him to the port of Aker. He sank his boat and made his way to the castle. Princian and Salome were in a hiding place that she thought was the

*The slavin (from Latin *sclavinia, sclavina*) was a cloak made from course wool that was worn by mendicants and pilgrims.

only place in the world where she would be safe from Marcolf. When the latter reached the castle gate, he got off his donkey and dragged himself toward the guard, who said: "So tell me, proud hero, how long have you been in this deplorable state?"

"Milord, I cannot remember precisely, but to tell the truth, I have been a cripple for some twenty years."

"You truly have a pitiful look about you. Would you like to get something to eat from the castle?"

"I am not hungry, but I would happily accept a drink."

"Wait here then! I'll bring you something."

He went down into the cellar, grabbed a valuable goblet, and brought it to Marcolf full of claret wine. While Marcolf drank, the porter sat next to him on a bench and told him: "Know, beggar, that a noble lady has arrived here by sea with King Princian but a short while ago. She is beautiful, attractive, and pale-skinned. You can be sure that she will not allow you to go away empty-handed. Look in the direction I am pointing. The queen is stuck inside a cave on that rocky isle because of a man named Marcolf, who wishes her ill."

"How is Princian able to meet her? Enlighten me!"

"I am going to tell you on condition you keep it secret. There is an underground passageway from my master's chamber that leads into the cave, which allows him to go to her. When he is with her, twelve of his best warriors guard the secret passageway."

"That has nothing to do with me. By the god you believe in, can you ask the king to come to the gate for a moment?"

The porter did as Marcolf asked.

Princian came out, accompanied by many knights. When Marcolf saw him, he tried to leap to his feet, but the king said to him: "No, stay put—you will hurt yourself! I will feed you as long as you live, if it pleases you to remain here."

"Look, Sire, how deformed my body is," said Marcolf, opening his pilgrim's cloak; "A doctor promised to cure me if I could pay him."

"I am going to give you three gold marks, and when you are healed, if you still need money, I will give you ten pounds."

Marcolf accepted the gift. Many knights were thronging to the castle gate to see the beggar and asking themselves how anyone could be so crippled. A chamberlain told Princian: "Sire, he is not as sick as he appears. If you allow me, I will cure him immediately." When Marcolf realized this plan, he discreetly took a plant from his pocket and put it in his mouth. It caused him to bloat so much that he looked to be on death's door. "You are deluded! If you wish to feel me, believe me, you will be convinced." The chamberlain came up and grabbed Marcolf's leg, trying to straighten it out, but the latter let out some powerful farts, freeing himself of the heathen, who was forced to jump back. "Beggar, you are right," he said. "You are crippled and sick. Your hands, your feet, your mouth, your eyes, your head, nothing is right with you—your brow alone is distinguished!* Knights, all of you should lend him assistance." Each dug into his purse and none of them gave him less than a gold pfennig.

Marcolf said, "I never had this in my hands before!" Princian gave

*The manuscripts provide two different readings: *hoffelich* ("courtly, distinguished") and *jemerlich* ("lamentable"); I have retained the first.

him a schilling. And the chamberlain added: "Forgive me for laying my hands on you."

After pocketing all this money, Marcolf added: "Powerful king, you have been so magnanimous toward me, but I will need a safe conduct so that your people do not rob me on my return trip." He then spotted a ring of red gold on the king's finger, in which someone had set a relic with great artistry, which moved him to tears.* The king took off his coat of mail but Marcolf said: "I cannot wear it, it is too precious for me, and if I lose it I will lose your favor forever. I would like something else from you, which I will return. I give you my word."

"What do you want, beggar?" Princian asked. "By the god in whose name you make this request, I shall gladly give it to you."

Marcolf pointed at the ring. "Even if it was worth a thousand marks, it would be for you," the king told him. "Hold out your hand, I will give it to you." Marcolf took it and bowed deeply before the relic while saying: "You have fulfilled my every wish, I shall never again be in want." His donkey was brought to him and the king personally helped him on to its back. Marcolf took his leave and was quite satisfied with his day's work, but he still could not resist playing one of his tricks. He tickled the donkey, which began running as fast as its legs could carry it and rushed with him into the deep moat of the castle. Princian and eleven of his men jumped in behind him and put him back in the saddle, but his leg was stuck and he let out three big farts, saying: "You have hurt me so badly I do not feel at all well."

"Get going and may your god protect you!" the king shouted.

Marcolf took the road that went across the country so that no one would suspect that he intended to travel by sea. However, at sunset he took a road leading to the coast. He hid his saddle and reins in the reeds, then went forward, quite pleased with himself. He spit out the magic plant and, as if by a miracle, recovered his health on the spot. As his plans included bringing a red silk robe, two fake beards,

*He recognized the ring that Solomon gave to his wife.

and a harp, he was able to evade all dangers. He put on a beard and some coarsely woven trousers, stuck an olive branch in his collar, and in the wink of an eye had transformed himself into a pilgrim. He cut a reed to use as a cane, and told his donkey: "I am leaving you in this grassy meadow, because I am going to Jerusalem alone."

When night fell, Princian returned to be with Salome, who asked him: "Sire, what did you do with your ring? It was my husband Solomon who gave it to me before I left him for the second time."

"Why should I have kept it? A poor wretch and unfortunate cripple came in search of me and begged me, in the name of my god, to give him a gift. A doctor was ready to treat him if he was able to pay for it. I gave him three gold marks; then he politely asked me for a safe conduct. I gave him my ring, but I think he will be dead tomorrow, for he was so ill."

"What did his eyes look like?" Salome asked, eager to know.

"They were as clear as a looking glass, and he had a distinguished brow."

"It is Marcolf, Solomon's vassal," cried the queen.

"Certainly not!" Princian retorted. "In Jerusalem I saw him wearing an ermine mantle. This man was a poor wretch, you can believe me."

"You do not know how cunning he can be! If you love me, send your warriors to block the exit at the port at once. Whoever brings this cripple to me will be given his weight in gold."

That very night two thousand soldiers locked the port down tight. Princian himself went in search of the cripple with a large troop of men and, as the story tells it, he did run across Marcolf.

"Tell me, pilgrim," he asked him, "Have you recently seen a cripple riding a well-fed donkey?"

"I saw him at sunset," Marcolf replied. "He told me he went to the king's home and was looking for a doctor. You will find his donkey at the edge of the road, a little farther down."

Princian gave him a schilling, saying: "This is for you, and if you come to my home, you will want for nothing." The heathens found the donkey, which they brought to Aker, but the inhabitants said they had never seen it. "The pilgrim who told me about the cripple, fooled me!" screamed Princian. "It must have been Marcolf, whom Solomon sent to spy on us." One of the heathens added: "Lead the animal to the queen and, if she recognizes it, then the pilgrim was clearly Marcolf," which was done. "I saw it in Jerusalem," said Salome, "where it carried stones every day for the construction of the temple. Keep watch on the port, for the pilgrim is Marcolf!"

During this time, Marcolf was preparing to leave. He removed his beard and trousers, hid his cane and sack in the reeds, put on a tunic of red silk, and picked up a German harp. These garments fit him elegantly, and he left disguised as a minstrel.[13]

A chamberlain at the castle had gathered fifty men together and set off in search of the pilgrim. He ran into—unbelievably enough—Marcolf in person and, when they stood facing each other, asked him: "Proud minstrel, tell me, have you come across a pilgrim?"

"At sunset I saw one going into Aker looking for an inn. He had a hairy beard and was wearing coarse trousers, and was well equipped for his pilgrimage. If you wish to wait here for a little while, you will surely see him pass by."

The chamberlain got down from his horse and Marcolf began playing his harp. The tunes were so enchanting that the other heathens also dismounted and the chamberlain, totally forgetting his mission, danced until the evening came.

"I must get to a feast and cannot linger any longer," Marcolf told them.

"Safe travels and may your god protect you; you are truly a fine minstrel," said the heathen, while giving him a schilling before returning from the city with his men to explain he had not found any pilgrim.

Salome questioned them: "Didn't you meet a man who told you about the pilgrim? That was Marcolf, I can assure you."

"Beautiful lady," the chamberlain responded, "you surprise me. Not everyone whose path you cross in the street is necessarily Marcolf! We certainly did run into a minstrel who was dressed elegantly. He played the German harp so well that it was truly enchanting."

"That was Solomon's vassal, Marcolf!" Salome exclaimed. "If you bring him to me here, I will give you thirty gold marks."

Marcolf was fully aware of Salome's shrewdness. He hid his harp and fine clothing, and put on a gray smock and a pair of large shoes. He then girded himself with a large belt, from which he hung a whetstone and a sharp knife. Equipped this way, he went into Aker: "Who has oxen? Who has sheep? I buy all!" An old heathen sold him some. Marcolf slaughtered them on the spot because he was in a hurry to skin them. The queen's men hunting for the minstrel questioned the butcher[14] to see if he might have seen a minstrel. Lowering his eyes, he answered: "Yes, I clearly saw a minstrel, but that is no trade for anyone with children to feed." He cut up a steer in small pieces and hailed the crowd: "Come here! Who would like to buy some meat? I will give you a good price!" The people thronged around him, and the queen's soldiers moved on. He remained in the city for three days and then decided it would be more prudent to change his disguise. "I am now going to make myself into a mercer," he said to himself. "Where will I be able to find lace and needles, belts, ribbons, pouches, and the red and green thread, with which women like to adorn themselves? Who will help me pull this off?" He purchased a stall and hurried to his hidden boat.* He then tossed his stall into the grass, saying, "May God help a poor man find you!" and then leaped joyfully into his skiff.

He returned to Jerusalem after a six-month absence and paid a visit to Solomon, who gave him a warm welcome in front of the entire court.

"I have found your wife," Marcolf told him. "Princian has hidden her in a secret place. We must steal her back from him!"

"Why did he hide her?" the king asked.

"Because he was scared of my maneuvers," Marcolf replied, before adding: "The secret apartment is located on a rocky island. A tunnel

*It so happens that he had sunk it in order to hide it.

makes it possible to get there, and Princian uses it to visit Salome."

"She has served the devil; may the devil go hunting for her!" Solomon exclaimed. "If I go with you, the same misadventure we had with Fore will happen again."

"You wish to abandon your wife, then?" asked Marcolf, laughing. "Did I just make this journey for nothing? Powerful king, you swore that I could kill her if I came back with her."

"When you bring her back, her fate will be in your hands."

"You casually gave her this," Marcolf said, showing Solomon the ring. "It was certainly ill-advised on your part, because what gives her the right to wear this relic? It was Princian who was wearing it, and I deftly recovered it from him. I promised to return it to him, and I must keep my word. Place three thousand men at my disposal and stay here. I will go back to the heathen kingdom with hopes that God grants me success and victory."

Duke Friedrich shouted out: "Marcolf, I am going to accompany you with one thousand warriors." These words elated Solomon, who then had boats made ready.

They sailed for two weeks or more before reaching Kastel, a mountain island where a mermaid lived[15] along with many wild dwarfs.[16]

They disembarked, glad to be done with this long crossing. The mermaid told her son: "Madelger, put on your invisibility-cloak* and go out in front of the mountain, because I smell the odor of German armor.† Marcolf has certainly arrived."

Madelger came out and spied Marcolf and a large troop. He took off his invisibility-cloak and said "Welcome, dear uncle,"‡ before taking him by the hand and leading inside the mountain, where the mermaid and her people gave him a warm welcome.

"Welcome to this heathen land!" she said. "It is surely King Solomon who has sent you to find his wife."

"My dearest aunt, advise me!"

"Even if thirty thousand warriors accompanied you, there is naught they could do. Dear nephew, you truly need my counsel."

"Help me take back the noble queen."

"Once night has fallen, I will send six dwarfs to destroy the tunnel beneath the mountain. Station yourself with twelve men beneath the window of the secret room and capture Princian and his cursed heathens."

Marcolf took his leave of her and informed his men, who then rested until the next day. At dawn, Marcolf made his way to the window of the secret chamber and yelled: "Are you there, noble King Princian? I am returning the ring you lent me and am keeping my promise!" When Salome heard him, she wept bitterly and moaned: "Marcolf is here! He has always wished me ill. Once he sees me, he will kill me."

"Calm down, noble lady!" Princian said, taking her by the hand to leave the premises, but they found the tunnel destroyed and were unable to pass through it. Marcolf entered the castle with his men, and then

---

*The term is *nebelkappe* (literally "fog cloak") in the text, also called a "hiding cloak" (*tarnkappe*), a magical garment that makes the wearer invisible.

†No explanation has ever been found for this phrase.

‡Uncle, aunt, and nephew are simply polite phrases here and do not imply any actual kinship.

the secret chamber. He captured Princian and many cursed heathens, whose lives were now under threat. He removed his ring, returned it to Princian, had a horse brought in, and held the stirrup out for him.* "Leave this place, king! The fact I am sparing your life is due to my magnanimity and nobility."

Princian sought refuge with his brother Belian and told him: "Help me, for I am in the depths of despair! My beautiful wife has been stolen, and my soldiers have been slain. Help me, brother, it is high time! Marcolf is the one to blame, you should know!"

"A brave man knows how to conceal his grief. You are behaving like a woman, Princian. Marcolf and his companions are dead men!"

That very night, Belian gathered together twelve thousand soldiers—a most powerful army! He had all the sea routes blockaded and presented himself before Marcolf. When he grasped the situation, he turned to his men and began haranguing them: "Brave heroes, we shall not retreat an inch! These are heathens; God has helped us on our journey up to now. He will reward our loyalty and allow us to return home." Duke Friedrich then declared: "With my glorious fighters, I will bring death to the enemy across this vast land!" An old and seasoned sergeant then spoke up: "I have already given the best I have to give before Troy and waged many battles. My sword has always hit its mark and will inflict countless wounds again today. Give me the standard! I am going to ride at the head of the army. Believe me, I will either lead you to death or victory!" The battle commenced and Duke Friedrich slew many heathens. Marcolf and the old sergeant wreaked so much havoc that they were wading through blood up to their spurs.

Belian charged at Marcolf and hit him so hard that he fell to his knees, but Marcolf got back up and, with one slash of his sword, split Belian's helmet and nose down to his teeth and the heathen fell dead to the ground. King Princian then threw himself into the battle with his

*This is traditionally a sign of vassalage.

warriors. The clangor of weapons swelled as blade clashed against blade. Fear and distress seized the heathens, bathing in their own blood. The confrontation lasted until vespers; then a truce was declared to allow the war-weary knights to rest.

The next morning, Marcolf planted himself in front of Princian's tent and asked: "Are you there, noble king? I challenge you to single combat! If you are victorious, you may keep Salome and let my people return to sea. And if the opposite is the case, I will allow your people to leave." They reached agreement and exchanged hostages before rushing upon each other. Princian let loose such a stroke at Marcolf that the latter collapsed and raised his hands toward the heavens, begging: "Lord God, save me! The sword blows have done me great harm. I am faithful to you; please do not let me die in a foreign land!" And God gave him a new burst of strength. Marcolf stood back up, saying: "Be on your guard, Princian! You are a dead man," and his sword struck him in the neck, causing his head to fly off. He picked it up and tossed it into Salome's lap: "Look, noble queen," he said to her. "This is your husband! What more can be said? If I bring you back to Jerusalem, you can be sure nothing will save you."

After the return of the Christian hostages, Marcolf had all the heathens slain, and they made haste to return to their boats. After

being away for half a year they arrived in Jerusalem, where Marcolf was given a warm welcome by Solomon and the entire court. He told the king: "Sire, after fooling around with another man, your wife must be cleansed!" The king gave his consent, and a bath was prepared in a marble tub. Once Salome had gotten into the bath, Marcolf knelt down next to her and gave her a cut, making her bleed. Once he had done this, he clasped her in his arms and smothered her. Then he had a cup brought in that he held up to her lips: "Noble queen, why do you refuse to drink with me! I will never offer you another."

When Solomon learned of the death of his wife, he sank into tears and said to Marcolf: "Pitiless and cruel man, why did you kill my beautiful wife?"

"She put me through much, day after day. By my faith, it is good I have put an end to it."

Salome was quickly carried to the cathedral, where she was placed in the casket she had lain in once before. "You will not escape this grave again until the Judgment Day," said Marcolf, who took Solomon by the hand and led him back to the palace.

Marcolf arranged for Solomon to marry Fore's sister, Affer. She ruled at his side over Jerusalem for thirty years as an all-powerful queen until the time God summoned them back to him.

📖 Karnein, ed. *Salman und Morolf.*

📖📖 Curschmann, *Spielmannsepik*; Kaplowitt, "The Heathens in Salman und Morolf"; Polczynska, *Studien zum "Salman und Morolf";* Schröder, *Spielmannsepik.*

six

Solomon and Marcolf

The Chapbook Illustrations

Marcolphus.
Frag vnnd ant
wort Künig Salo=
monis/vnd Mar=
colphi.

Gedruckt zů Straßburg am Roßmarckt
bey Christian Müller.

Published in Strasbourg in 1550, the chapbook does not illustrate the same scenes of the story as did the earlier manuscript because public tastes had changed. The scene of Solomon's famous judgment is a new addition. Marcolfus (Marcolf) no longer slips into an oven but instead into a hole, the king's fickle wife is not featured, and so on.

How the captain of the king addressed Marcolfus

How King Solomon set off on the hunt. One of his servants shows him the house of Marcolfus

Marcolfus brings Solomon a jug of milk

How the King and Marcolfus kept vigil all night long

Here Marcolfus shares with the king everything he thought during the night

How Marcolfus accused his sister

Marcolfus lets a mouse out of his sleeve
and it runs on the table

Marcolfus frees a hare and the
dogs leap after it in pursuit

Two women come forth with
a dead child and a living child

Now you understand how women
come in and debate

Marcolfus crawls on all fours

Marcolfus spits on the bald man's forehead

Solomon and his servants come to the hole into which Marcolfus has slipped

Marcolfus is brought out to be hung

The servants bring Marcolfus back and recount what happened

Seven

Štilfríd and Bruncvík (*Old Czech*)

Distinguishing itself from the legend of Henry the Lion, Duke of Brunswick,[1] *the story of Štilfríd and Bruncvík has come down to us in five fifteenth-century manuscripts. They bear different titles,*[2] *and the story was even translated into Russian.*[3] *There are two different versions, one of which is transmitted in a manuscript from the Prague University library and the other through a number of popular chapbooks. The oldest chapbook dates from 1565 and was printed in Olomouc by Job Günther.*

A prince named Štilfríd lived in Bohemia. He was very enterprising and always carried his plans out to completion. His wife was named Theodora, and she was the daughter of a Lombard king. She gave birth to a son, whom her husband named Bruncvík. From his earliest youth this lad showed himself to be the worthy successor of his father. After a certain time, Štilfríd wished to fulfill a plan he had long been thinking about. He wanted to leave so he could become acquainted with his land and its language. He also wished to replace the cauldron that was depicted on his coat of arms with an eagle. He therefore took leave of his wife and set out, accompanied by only a single servant. He traveled through many kingdoms without Štilfríd ever finding his equal, and he finally came to the court of the King Astronomus of Naples, who gave him a friendly reception. The sovereign became friends with this adventurous knight, who served him zealously, which is the reason why he was awarded much favor and many honors.

Time went by until one day Astronomus received a missive from King Filosofus, who ruled over England or Mesopotamia [*sic*], a missive that contained the worst kind of threats. Astronomus was quite distressed by this and fell into despair, but Štilfríd gave him encouragement and urged him to set off to war. Astronomus therefore raised an army and sent his foe a message suggesting that each of them choose two thousand horses, and that each of these horses would carry one thousand silver marks. Filosofus would then have to select twelve of his best warriors, who would confront just one of his men. The victor would not only win the money carried by the horses, but also the kingdom of his enemy. Filosofus gladly accepted this deal, fully convinced that the valor of his fighters would prevail. Although Štilfríd had told him he would personally battle the other king's chosen warriors, the king of Naples was still anxious about the outcome of the battle.

On the day that had been set, many lords and princes took their places at the battleground and all was arranged in the manner they had agreed. The names of the king of England's warriors were Simforian zLevsdtftu; Lipolt, duke of Austria; Rudolf; Typartit, a Greek duke; the margrave Theobaldus; Tristram of Opočan; Pitopas zMezirhadí; Adrian, an African lord; Brunda, the margrave of Tas; Benedict, the prince of Tyr; Nederšpan, a Hungarian lord; and Žibrid (Siegfried), prince of Tennemark.* For his part, Štilfríd had had twelve banners made. One was white with a gold cross and had the name of Saint Wenzel, the others were green, red, yellow, blue, purple, violet, pale yellow, gray, and a scarlet banner on which a lion had been painted.† He held one of these

*This appears to be a reference to Sigfried of Denmark, that is to say, Sigurðr of Germanic legend.

†This is an inconsistency on the author's part: only ten banners are described.

banners during each duel and thereby vanquished his twelve courageous adversaries, one after the other, to the great dismay of the king of England, who had promised his men goods and favors, as well as the hand of his daughter and half of his kingdom if they were victorious and humiliated this boastful knight. Astronomus thanked Štilfríd, and was ready to grant him whatever he wished as a reward, but the warrior asked only to be recognized as the prince of Bohemia and for permission to replace the cauldron against a background of flames on his coat of arms with a black eagle on a gold field, to which the king gladly assented.

The king of England had met with Štilfríd and Astronomus to hand over his kingdom in conformance with their agreement, but they allowed him to keep it on condition he never again wage war on them.

Štilfríd then thought of returning home as he greatly desired to see his wife and child, whom he had not seen for three years, and none of the pleas of Astronomus could hold him back. The king gave him rich gifts and granted him leave, but accompanied him to Bohemia. On his entry into Prague, Štilfríd was joyfully welcomed by his family. His first act was to have an eagle painted over all the gates to the city. When he saw young Bruncvík, Astronomus promised the lad the hand of his daughter Neomenia,* and then returned to his own land. On his return he sent the Napolitan princess to Prague, where she was solemnly wed to Bruncvík. When he died, Štilfríd left him all his worldly goods, and all of Bohemia went through a long period of mourning for their prince.

Bruncvík then ruled, following the example of his father. After two years had passed, he began thinking of his father's deeds and decided to imitate them. He set himself the goal of replacing the eagle his father had acquired for their coat of arms with a lion.† He told his wife Neomenia that he wanted to set off on adventure and obtained her consent, despite her grief, and they exchanged rings. "You should not believe what the bearer of news might present to you. Wait for me for

*In Greek the name means "New Moon."

†During the Middle Ages, a person's coat of arms would evolve over the course of its owner's life and serve as a reminder of his life's path.

seven years, and if I have not returned by that time, you may remarry, as I will be dead and that ring shall turn black." Neomenia broke down in tears and began moaning.

"Who will protect me? My mother and father are a long way away from here!"

"It is just as hard for me to leave you," Bruncvík answered, "but my decision to leave is final."

She tried to dissuade him by all means available, but he remained steadfast. After he had put all his affairs in order and taken leave of his beautiful Neomenia, he set off for foreign lands with thirty steeds, riding until he reached the sea. With his men, he took a boat, filled it with provisions, and set out on the open seas. They sailed for three months without reaching land, until one night when a violent storm tossed their vessel toward the Magnetic Mountain (*hora Akštyn*).[4] When they came close, it pulled them—as was its nature—to a nearby island, called Zelator, meaning the "Island of the Blessed." There they saw countless boats that had foundered there with their entire crews, and they complained bitterly about the fate awaiting them because all their attempts to get free were in vain. They began to starve and, with cries of despair, they slaughtered their horses. One day, while he was strolling around the island, Bruncvík met a strange being who was half woman and half fish,[5] named Europa, and she gave him his full pleasure. As their hunger had become even more cruelly felt, Bruncvík's companions began devouring one another until at last the only people remaining were Bruncvík himself and his faithful servant Balad, who had decided to sacrifice his own life for his master. "You should leave this place and go home to your wife! The griffin[6] can pull you free of this trap!" he told him. Following his servant's advice, Bruncvík allowed himself to be sewn inside a horse's hide sprinkled with blood. A ferocious griffin lunged upon this prey and seized it in its claws, before carrying it off to his nest beyond the sea. The griffin's young welcomed him with cheeps of joy and hurled themselves upon this feast, but—and this is the truth—know that Bruncvík defended himself by killing them with his sword. He then climbed down from the nest. Dreading the return of the griffin, he headed off at random in the wild and desolate country around the nest, and wandered among the bleak mountains for a long time. Eleven days and eleven nights later, he came upon a charming valley where he ate delicious fruits. But all at once he heard a terrible racket and spotted a lion grappling with a nine-headed dragon[7] that was breathing fire.[8] While commending his fate to God, he hurled himself atop the monster because the lion had found itself in a perilous position. The noble animal withdrew to the side to recover its strength while Bruncvík dealt some fierce blows and cut off six of the beast's heads. The lion then joined him in the battle again, and together they eventually slew the dragon.

Bruncvík resumed his journey, but the lion remained by his side, not wishing to leave him.[9] Fearful of the animal's strength and prowess, the duke attempted to sneak away from him. Wounded by his distrust, the lion redoubled his shows of friendship by hunting for Bruncvík, but his savior could not let go of his anxiety. Equipping himself with acorns and beechnuts, he climbed into a tree to wait for the beast to grow weary and leave. He remained sitting on a branch for three days while the lion, lying at the foot of the tree, kept his eye on the knight, showing how grieved he was by Bruncvík's behavior. He roared so loud that the earth and the tree shook. In terror, Bruncvík lost his grip and fell from the tree, seriously hurting himself. The lion brought him a plant that caused Bruncvík to regain his senses, and the beast was overjoyed by the sight of his master's recovery. From that moment on, Bruncvík looked at the animal with another eye. Seeing that the hero was hungry, the lion went hunting and brought back some game for him, which he cooked with his burning hot breath. This helped him win the knight's trust.

Bruncvík then resumed his journey again, traveling through wild, deserted forests. He walked for a long time and then scaled a mountain, on which he climbed up a tree to get a look at the surrounding area. He spotted a castle on an island in the middle of the sea, which gave him hope. He addressed a brief prayer to God, asking for his assistance, and then, once on the shore, he built a raft out of wood and twigs. Taking advantage of the absence of the lion, who was off hunting, he set a course for the island.[10] When he returned to the beach with a wild boar, the lion saw Bruncvík pulling away. He leaped into the water with his prey and caught up to the raft as it was sailing between the dark cliffs of Mount Karbunkulus. While he was making this passage, Bruncvík found a red carbuncle.

They disembarked near the castle, and terror took hold of the hero when he saw that the surrounding area was swarming with monsters of every kind. They made their way to the home of King Olibrius, who had eyes in front and in back, eighteen fingers on each hand, eighteen toes on each foot, and was surrounded by extremely misshapen creatures:[11] some had naught but one foot or one eye, some had horns, while others had two heads or the heads of dogs.[12] Others were half gray and half white, or were humped like camels or ruddy like foxes. All of them were making a hellish din. Bruncvík started to turn back, but Olibrius spoke to him:

"Bruncvík, we are fully aware of who you are. Do you come here of your own free will or out of obligation? I ask you this for we have never seen men like you here before."

"Gracious sovereign," the gallant knight responded, "I left my country of my own free will, but I have arrived here under duress and constraint."

"I believe you. You can help me if you deliver my daughter Afrika, whom the horrible dragon Basiliskus* has abducted and imprisoned in his castle in Arabia. If you succeed, I will help you return home."

Bruncvík was dumbstruck on seeing that the king knew his name and decided to take on this adventure.

"If you keep your word and let me cross through the iron gate,"[13] he replied, "I will go free her."

*This dragon would therefore be a basilisk: the king of serpents, whose gaze causes petrifaction.

"I give you my promise!" Olibrius replied.

Three days later Bruncvík had his boat equipped, which had been laden with five months' worth of provisions, and he set sail with the lion. When they reached the castle of Basiliskus, which had three gates, they spied two terrible monsters near the first one keeping guard, bound by iron chains. These horrors had human heads, the bodies of horses, and the tails of pigs. They were called Monetrus. Bruncvík engaged them in a long combat and, with the help of the lion, ended up slaying them.

Near the second gate two other monsters were stationed; they were even stronger and were called Glato. Each of them had two horns that were two ells in length* and sharp as razors. When they fought, these beasts had the custom of folding one horn over their back while they used the other so they could change them when the first horn had become blunt.† The only thing that gave them fright was the color red. Bruncvík engaged them in bitter combat and, with the help of the lion, eventually slew them.

The third gate was guarded by two beasts that were the most terrifying of all. They belonged to a species called Sidforove. They had the claws of bears, the horns of devils, black teeth that looked like those of horses, and a mouth so huge that a full-grown man would be naught but a mouthful. If God and the lion had not helped him, Bruncvík surely would have perished.

Once he had gotten rid of these terrifying gatekeepers, Bruncvík entered the castle with its luxurious furnishings and immense riches. When he entered the great hall, he saw a beautiful maiden who was a woman to the waist, but whose legs were replaced by the bodies of serpents. When she caught sight of Bruncvík, she asked him:

"Bruncvík, how did you get here?"

"Your father Olibrius sent me to free you, sweet Afrika."

*[An ancient unit of measure based on the forearm (ca. 45 inches). —*Ed.*]

†This would be the *yale,* about which Solinus says: "When the yale fights, it points one of its horns forward and folds the other back, so that if the tip of the first one becomes blunted, the other can take its place" (*Collectanea rerum memorabilium,* 52, 34).

"O dear Bruncvík, even if someone possessed the strength of a thousand men, they could not defeat the monstrous gatekeepers! Tell me, they must have been asleep since you are here unscathed?"

"Yes, as for sleeping, they are sleeping."

"Then take advantage of their slumber to flee before they wake up and tell my father that I am doing fine!"

"No, whatever the cost, I shall free you!"

This statement inflamed Afrika with love. She approached him, embraced him, and gave him a ring that bestowed its wearer with the strength of twenty-four men. Then she said: "From noon to evening, I am compelled to have these serpent bodies for my legs,* but I regain my original appearance through the night until the following noon. The dragon Basiliskus comes to see me at three o'clock in the afternoon and rests in my lap. Get out! He will not be long in returning."

Bruncvík commended his fate to God when he heard the monster approaching in a terrifying racket, surrounded by all manner of reptiles and a mob of other malevolent creatures. Although he was swimming in venom up to his nostrils, the valiant knight wreaked vast carnage, and his lion did not remain on the sidelines! The battle lasted all night until the following noon. The exhausted Bruncvík was on the verge of defeat when his faithful lion tore the dragon to pieces. Weakened from blood loss and countless wounds, the hero fell to the ground unconscious and remained that way for three days and three nights, to the great despair of Afrika. The lion returned holding medicinal plants in its mouth that he gave Bruncvík to eat[14] and, nine days later, the knight was fully recovered.

They transported as much wealth as they could carry to the boat and brought the young woman back to her father Olibrius, who pressured Bruncvík to marry her. Some time passed, during which the prince of Bohemia never stopped searching for a means to escape. One night, when he was unable to sleep, he explored the castle and stumbled

*This brings to mind the legend of the Himantopodes, whose legs look like straps.

upon an ancient sword in a hall. He was seduced by its excellent quality and he swapped it for his own. The following night, he asked Afrika about it.

"Would you tell me a secret if I asked you to?"

"You know well that I am unable to refuse you anything," she replied. "Ask me!"

"So just what is that mysterious sword that is hanging in a hall?"

In response, Afrika put him to sleep, leaped out of bed, and went to seal the weapon behind nine locks, but it was too late! When she returned, she awoke her husband and said:

"I am completely surprised that you were able to see that sword that no one until now has managed to see and which once belonged to an ancient knight. If you knew its properties, you would be amazed!"

"So what are they?" asked Bruncvík, who had to repeat his demand several times before he learned what they were.

"I will explain it to you," Afrika said reluctantly. "If you unsheathe it while saying 'one head, two heads, ten, twenty, thirty, one hundred, one thousand heads cut off,' that will happen immediately."*[15] Bruncvík experimented with the sword by slaying several monsters that entered his chamber.† When Olibrius, his daughter, and all the monstrous inhabitants of the castle were seated at the dinner table, he pulled the sword from its scabbard, wished that all there would be decapitated, and all their heads rolled across the floor. He gathered together all the jewels and other riches that he could find, carried them to a boat, opened the iron gate that was the only one that would allow him to flee that region, and set off with his faithful lion.

After he had been sailing for some time, an island named Tripatrita came into view. He could hear the sound of trumpets and drums, as well as joyous singing coming from the isle. He brought his boat to shore and he spotted groups on foot and on horseback who were entertaining

*Variant: "If someone looks at it, he will become petrified."

†Variant: "He took a walk along the shore and encountered sea monsters that he killed with his sword."

themselves in a thousand ways. A person approached him and invited him to join them while holding out his hand. When Bruncvík took it, he almost burned himself on it. He pulled out his sword and slew the burning creature, but the others came running toward him. They were the devils of Asmodeus (*Azmodeowe diabli*), who were imprisoned on this island as punishment. They met the same fate as their fellow creature.

Bruncvík put back out to sea and continued his journey. He spent fifteen weeks wandering through a host of perils before eventually discovering a large city far from everything. This was Egbatanis,* a city filled with splendid dwellings, yet all were deserted though the tables in each of them were set and meals were waiting ready to be served. The inhabitants, the Astryolowe, soon returned, however, and Bruncvík saw that they all had only one eye in the center of their foreheads. They brought the gallant knight before King Astriolus, who tried to extort the promise from Bruncvík to remain there forever. If he refused, they would sit him upon Rosa, a fiery horse, astride which he would remain for all eternity. Bruncvík refused. Astriolus ordered Rosa brought forward, and four of his men approached the hero to perch him on the beast, but Bruncvík drew his sword and slew them. Astriolus then put an army of one thousand men to oppose him, but the hero shouted out: "Twenty, thirty, one hundred, one thousand heads to the ground!" and immediately the din caused by falling heads hitting the ground caused the earth to shake. In terror, Astriolus begged Bruncvík to stop massacring his men and promised to lead him back to his own land with his lion and all his belongings.

The king and our prince set sail, and, after a long voyage, Astriolus left Bruncvík on the outskirts of Prague with all his weapons and baggage. The prince disguised himself as a pilgrim and made his way into the city where he strolled about, the center of attention because of his lion. The inhabitants were delighted and cried out: "What a huge beast!" He learned that King Astronomus was planning this very day to

*This old Assyrian city, Εκβάτανα (Ecbatana) in Greek, is presented here as a place of geographical wonders.

wed his daughter Neomenia to Kleofas, an Assyrian prince. He made his way to the castle, where he left his lion at the gate so he would not be recognized, as he was certain that Neomenia would recall what he said to her when they parted. He entered and experienced great anguish at the sight of his wife sitting next to Kleofas. Libations were made after the meal was over, and someone handed Bruncvík the cup from which the newlyweds had drunk. He slipped his ring inside of it, left the palace, and wrote over its gate: "I have returned after my seven-year absence." Neomenia recognized his ring and warned her father, but Kleofas overheard her and set off in pursuit of Bruncvík with thirty of his knights to kill him. When he saw them approaching, the hero unsheathed his sword and shouted out: "Off with the heads of the fiancé and his men!" Their heads flew off, the lion tore their bodies to pieces, and their now riderless horses returned to the city.

Bruncvík then went to one of his castles where he summoned the lords of Bohemia to his side and left with them for Prague. Neomenia and Astronomus came to meet them with numerous townspeople, both young and old, all jubilant at the sight of their prince's return with a lion. Bruncvík described his adventures and then had a lion painted, his new coat of arms, over the gates of the city and on his banner. He reigned for forty-five years and had a son named Ladislav, to whom he bequeathed his kingdom when he died at a ripe old age. The lion could not bear to go on living without him and died of grief.

Glory to God in the highest heaven!

Dvê kroniky, o Stylfrydovi druhä o Brunevfkovi
(Two Chronicles of Štilfríd and Bruncvík;
sixteenth century)

📖 Černá, *Povídka o Bruncvíkovi*; Erben, ed., *Wýbor z literatury české,* vol. II, 39–74; Petrovskij, ed., *История о славном короле Брунцвике* (Istoriâ o slavnom korole Bruncvíke); Polivká, *Kronika o Bruncvíkovi v ruské literatuře*; Voborník, *Dvě kroniky o Štilfrídovi a Bruncvíkovi.*

📖📖 Baumann, *Die Sage von Heinrich dem Löwen bei den Slaven;* Lecouteux, "Herzog Ernst" v. 2164ff; Sárdi, "Von Braunschweig bis Bruncvik."

by way of conclusion

The Priest Amis, an Adventurer

(*Middle High German*)

Der Pfaffe Amis *(The Adventures of the Priest Amis)*[1] *recounts—in twelve episodes and 2,510 lines—the life of its eponymous hero, a charlatan, who sets off from England and wanders through France, Lorraine, and Greece*

in a variety of disguises. Sometimes he is a cleric, sometimes he is a painter, and sometimes a merchant or physician. His dupes come from all levels of society: from king to peasant and from bishop to monk.

First written down by Der Stricker, a name that literally means "the Knitter" (implying a knitter of tales), Der Pfaffe Amis *enjoyed great popularity, and some episodes from it were used again by Hermann Bote*[2] *(1467–1520), the city scribe of Brunswick, in his* Dil Ulenspeigel (Till Eulenspiegel).[3]

1. THE INVISIBLE FRESCO

This story, which is of Eastern origin, can also be found in the Libro de los enxiemplos del conde Lucanor et de Patronio *by the Castilian prince Don Juan Manuel (1284–1348).*[4] *Hans Christian Andersen follows the same basic outline in his story called "The Emperor's New Clothes" (Kejserens ny klæder).*

Now a man of wealth, the priest Amis had become swollen with pride and, not wishing to stop in the middle of a good thing, left for France. When he arrived in Paris, he presented himself before the king and said:

"I would be most honored if you had need of any of my talents."

"Tell me, Master, what art have you mastered?" the sovereign asked.

"I paint so skillfully that all sing my praises. I have a particular technique that no one but I possesses, for I invented it, Milord. I paint frescos both on houses and on great halls. I paint scenes on the wall that recall everything that humanity has seen and experienced. When my task is complete, I invite the noble ladies and lords, and their retinues, to come see them. Young or old, none are skilled or educated enough to see them—except those who have the good fortune of being their parent's legitimate children. They alone and nobody else! Children that have been born out of wedlock will not see the slightest brushstroke. If you would like such a work, I stand ready to prove to you that I am the master of this technique."

"Most gladly," replied the monarch, who led Amis into the hall of a splendid building—it was quite tall and vast—and invited the priest to examine it, and he asked him what salary he would demand for painting it.

"You have been highly praised as a noble person in many ways," our priest responded, "it will be easy for you to pay me 300 marks. My expenses are so high that my final profit is quite meager."

"If you want more, you will have it before we part, and I beg you to finish the fresco quickly. I have never spent any money more willingly."

"With my technique," Amis then told him, "no one should enter the hall. I plan to have finished the work in six weeks at the most. Forbid everyone from entering here in the meantime; it is under these conditions that I will paint your hall."

"I give you my promise! Shut the door tight. Two guards will stand watch and not allow anyone to enter before me. I am going to go away with my vassals. On my return, I will give you a property, and each knight wishing to enter here should give you a gift. If all goes as expected, they must present themselves so that we may learn who is an illegitimate child. By God, I will dispossess those individuals of their fiefs!"

On this note, the sovereign left with his knights and had his decision made known.

With his assistants, the priest Amis entered the hall and began to paint. Let us take a look at how he went about this! He covered the windows and refused entry to all people except for his assistants. He was generously provided with all he desired, meat, fish, mead, and wine. And here is what he did: he lazed about without painting a stroke! He lived in the great hall until the deadline had come and the king had returned with his knights. No one had been allowed to turn down his invitation, so he was accompanied by everyone he had met during the time that had passed while he was away from his palace. His arrival was hardly what would be called discreet! Master Amis came out of the hall, greeted the king, and invited him to enter, adding: "Leave the knights outside until I know whether my work has pleased you, and I have explained the images to you." Delighted, the monarch entered, closing the door behind him.

Filled with impatience, he contemplated the walls without seeing anything more than before because nothing had been painted. He examined the entire room and felt as if he was drowning in grief; hadn't he personally asked for it to be painted? "I have lost my honor doubly," he said to himself, "my own and that of my mother. If I admit I cannot see anything, those who do see something will see that I was born out of wedlock. I am blind because I am illegitimate! That the noble ladies, knights, and even the squires can come contemplate these images while I can see nothing, upsets me greatly and deals me an almost mortal blow." Turning to Amis, he said:

"Master, explain to me what you have depicted so wonderfully.

"Here is Solomon and his father David," said Amis; "the quarrel between Absalom and David when David was pursuing him and Absolom's hair became caught by a branch that had left him hanging there. The other fresco shows Alexander the Great victorious over Darius and Poros, the king of the Indies, as well as other deeds of the Macedonian hero. And here, sire, are the mighty feats of the Roman kings. You can see what Babylon was like before God punished it by confusing the languages. But what I painted over there speaks only of you. I have depicted you surrounded by your knights sitting and

standing, and I have shown the grief of those who cannot see anything.

"Now I can see all of that quite clearly,"[5] stated the king with aplomb. "May whoever sees nothing deal with it as best he can! For my own part, I have never seen a more admirably decorated hall."

"Very well, bid your vassals to enter," replied Amis, "and explain to them how I should be rewarded."

The sovereign opened the door and proclaimed: "May each knight entering here reward the artist, otherwise he must remain outside! I have promised him this source of profit." All came forward; some gave a piece of armor or money, others a horse or a sword. This was how Amis was able to enrich himself and gain in influence. Jostling one another for place, the knights entered the hall. All were dismayed when they saw nothing, and in order to keep their honor they all stated that the frescos were superb. All of them felt their hearts sinking and looked downcast because they were afraid of losing their fiefdoms and being ruined because of their inability to see. When they heard the king explain that they had to look at this and that, thereby repeating the words of Amis, they all nodded in agreement and looked downcast because they could see their dishonor. Each of them would have sworn they were the only one to see nothing but assured the others they saw it perfectly, and more than one were annoyed at their mothers for not taking better care of their honor. When everyone had looked and publicly stated that these paintings were masterpieces, Amis implored the king to give him permission to leave and to pay him his salary, which he obtained at once. He bid his farewells and left. Fortune had looked upon him with such favor that he had pocketed an additional two hundred marks from the court. He sent them home to England with the express wish that they treat his guests well during his absence.

Once the knights had contemplated the hall at their leisure, the queen and her ladies presented themselves the next day to view the frescoes. Imagine their fright when they realized they could see nothing, but they reacted as everyone before them had and claimed the opposite. Finally, the squires came in who shamelessly declared that these paintings were extremely beautiful and that they had never before seen anything so wondrous, but one of them who was a simpleton said: "If you could really see them, then I would see them, too, for my eyes are not made of glass!" Then all those who were shamed by his words retorted: "What we do understand is that you can't see anything, so you must be an illegitimate child!"

"I don't know whose son I am," the simpleton replied, "but whatever I am, those walls are totally lacking any paintings! Anyone claiming the contrary has to fight with me."

The squires argued for some time, until a majority of them stated that they could not see anything and anyone who said otherwise was crazy. The wisest among them said the simpleton was right and ended by praising his truthfulness.

When the knights joined them and heard what they were saying, they began arguing, but truth ultimately prevailed over lies and they all spoke unanimously—except for the king—that they had been deceived. The monarch held his tongue and thought what words would best be fit for replying. Once everyone had stated that the walls were bare, he admitted that he thought the same thing. There was an explosion of laughter and a huge racket, over which he said, "This priest is a cunning fox to have made his fortune this way!"

2. PRIEST AMIS THE DOCTOR

After the priest Amis had acquired so much money and things from the court of France, he left for Lorraine and asked to meet the duke, who immediately granted his request. He told him that, with the exception of God, there was no better physician than him.[6]

"You have been sent to me by God," the duke responded, "and I rejoice at your coming. I have relatives and vassals here whose suffering affects me greatly. Many are bedridden and at the brink of death. If God helps you to heal them, your fortune is made."

"I am such a good doctor," Amis explained, "that I can heal all those who are ill, except for lepers and the wounded. Even if they were afflicted by the most serious diseases, and even if they numbered more than one thousand, I would heal them before the end of the day. I want to take nothing, neither gifts nor money, before you have seen them healed and their healing has been confirmed to you from their own mouths. It is only then that you will pay me."

The duke was quite satisfied at this and said: "Your words please me greatly."

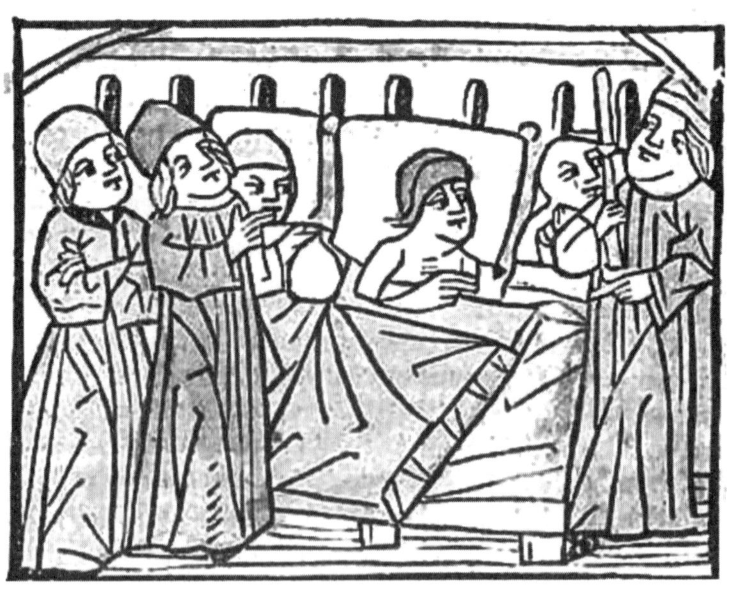

People were sent out to find patients and soon twenty of them had arrived. Amis led them into a separate room and told them: "In a few moments, you will have fully recovered if you promise to keep quiet about my healing methods for an entire week before revealing them. This is the first step for getting your health back."

They allowed themselves to be convinced and promised to keep the secret. Amis then went on to say: "Go away and decide among yourselves which is the sickest one among you. You will then tell me who you have designated and will be cured soon after, for I will kill that person and his blood will allow me to heal you, for which my own head stands as a surety."

The patients then grew scared! One of them, who could barely walk, feared that if his disability was seen it would sign his death warrant. He therefore went to the deliberation without his cane. Let us take a look at what reactions Amis's statement had caused! Each of the patients said: "I can minimize my problem, but someone else will say that his health problem is even less significant, and someone else will say that his is even less serious. In the end, they will all say that I am the sickest of them all, and they will kill me and heal themselves. As a precaution I will say that I am only slightly stricken by illness." All shared the same thought, which was why they told the priest Amis that, by a miracle, they were completely healed.[7] "You are lying," he replied to them. Each of them swore on their honor that it was the truth. Their doctor was most satisfied by their words. "Go tell it to the duke!" he commanded them, which they did at once. They told their lord that a saint had appeared to them and that they had recovered their health.[8] Greatly astonished, the duke interrogated each of them individually, seeking to learn the truth. As they were bound by the promise they had made to the priest, they revealed nothing to him. The duke immediately commanded one hundred marks be brought out for Amis; no one opposed him, and the sum was weighed out.* The duke gave Amis his

*To verify that the money was good.

blessing and allowed him to leave. Amis had the money sent to England with the order to share it equally among his guests.

A week after his departure, the patients, still feeling as poorly as before if not worse, then came forward and explained to the duke the way in which the doctor had tricked them, and how he had extorted the oath to reveal nothing of it for a week from them. When the duke learned the truth, he shared it with his entourage.

An enormous burst of laughter shook the entire court of Lorraine, as it had earlier in France, and all acknowledged that Amis was a wily rascal.

This adventure, akin to the Old French fabliau of the Vilain mire *(thirteenth century), can be also found in the* Liber Facetiarum *(Book of Jests) by Poggio Bracciolini (1380–1459) under the title "Xenodochium," and Molière mined the same vein in his farce* Le Médecin malgré lui *(The Physician in Spite of Himself).*

📖📖 Haupt, "Der Pfaffe amis und Ulenspiegel"; Könneker, "Strickers Pfaffe Amis und das Volksbuch von Ulenspiegel."

Notes

INTRODUCTION. BETWEEN THE WORLDS

1. Adam of Bremen, *Gesta Hammaburgensis Ecclesiae Pontificum,* IV, 40.
2. Cf. Lecouteux, "Zur Vermittlung mittelalterlicher sagenhafter Erzählstoffe."
3. Heidlauf, ed., *Lucidarius,* I, 13, 4–14.
4. Werber, *Les Thanatonautes.*
5. Gaudé, *La Porte des enfers.*

1. JOURNEYS TO THE BORDERLANDS

1. Motif F 531: *Giant.*
2. Alexander wants to know if it is a beast or a human; cf. Ryssel, "Die syrische Übersetzung des Pseudo-Kallisthenes," 263, and the Serbian version (Christians, *Die serbische Alexandreis,* 261). Motif G 11.2: *Cannibal giant.*
3. The same thing is found in the Syriac translation (Ryssel, "Die syrische Übersetzung des Pseudo-Kallisthenes," 364), as well as in the Armenian (Raabe, ed., *Die armenische Übersetzung der sagenhaften Alexanderbiographie,* 71) and Latin translations (Feldbusch, *Der Brief Alexanders an Aristoteles,* 55a).
4. Motif F 511.0.1: *Headless person.* For more on acephalic beings, cf. Lecouteux, *Les Monstres dans la littérature allemande du Moyen Âge,* 377–81.
5. Cf. motif A 692: *Islands of the blest.*
6. Motif N 825.2: *Old man helper.*
7. Motif F 706: *Land of darkness.*

8. For more on this legend, cf. Pandler, *Die Volkserzählungen von der Abschaffung der Altentötung,* 22ff.
9. Motif H 1376.7: *Quest for immortality.* This water of life makes an earlier appearance in the *Epic of Gilgamesh* (ca. 3000 BCE). Herodotus mentions it in his *Histories* (III, 23); and it can also be found in the Babylonian Talmud (cf. Friedlaender, *Die Chadhirlegende und der Alexanderroman,* 42–50), and in a homily by the Syriac bishop, Jacob of Serugh (Friedlaender, *Die Chadhirlegende,* 50).
10. Motif V 230: *Angels.*
11. A variant version has: "You are called Kalé the beautiful, I henceforth name you the Beautiful One of the mountain, because that is where you live." Motif D 199.3: *Transformation: woman to siren.*
12. Motif D 95: *Transformation: man to demon.*
13. These are griffins; cf. Lecouteux, *Les Monstres dans la allemande du Moyen Âge,* 625–34.
14. Motif B 552: *Man carried by bird.*
15. Motif V 230: *Angels.* For more on this flight, cf. Settis-Frugoni, *Historia Alexandri elevati per griphos ad aerem.* Alexander's adventure brings to mind that of Etana, the main character of a Sumerian story in which he tries to reach heaven. Alexander's aerial flight was frequently depicted in medieval art, for example, in a sculpture on the Cathedral of Fidenza in Emilia-Romana, Italy, and an archway relief at the Parish Church of Saints Peter and Paul in Remagen, Germany.
16. Thalabi, *Kitāb Qīsas al-Anbijā al-Musamma' bi'l 'rā'is,* Cairo, 1314h.
17. I am translating from Friedlaender's text, *Die Chadhirlegende,* 162–71.
18. Cf. motif F 403.2.2.2: *Angels as familiar spirits.*
19. Motif E 80: *Water of life.*
20. Motif F 706: *Land of darkness.*
21. Twelve months, according to another source; cf. Friedlaender, *Die Chadhirlegende,* 154.
22. In the Ethiopian version of the legend, the bird is found in a room that is encircled by a band of iron; cf. Budge, *The Life and Exploits of Alexander the Great,* 273.
23. On the angel Israfil, cf. Fahd, "Anges, démons et djinns en Islam."
24. This concerns the legend that is known in the West as the "stone of paradise"; cf. Lecouteux, *Mondes parallèles,* 25–33.
25. Budge, *The Life and Exploits of Alexander the Great,* 276: rubies and crystals.

26. Cf. Pliny, *Historia naturalis,* VIII, 27.
27. Nearchus, a navarch of Alexander's fleet in 325, said that they have nails like claws, which they use to tear open fish (fragment 24 in Jacoby, *Fragmente der griechischen Historiker,* 688); in the Syriac version, they have the faces of horses (Ryssel, "Die syrische Übersetzung des Pseudo-Kallisthenes," 71).
28. Motif D 1610.2: *Speaking tree.*
29. Cf. the Valley of Diamonds in the *Second Voyage of Sinbad the Sailor* from the tales of *The One Thousand and One Nights.*
30. In the Syriac version, they contain fifty measures of water; cf. Raabe, ed., *Die armenische Übersetzung der sagenhaften Alexanderbiographie,* 369.
31. In the Syriac version, they weigh twenty pounds.

2. JOURNEYS TO THE OTHERWORLD

1. Motif F 377.1: *Supernatural lapse of time in paradise.* Odo of Cheriton (*Parabolae,* no. 780) speaks of two hundred years; Jacques de Vitry (*Exempla,* no. 19), Johannes Pauli (*Schimpf und Ernst,* no. 562), and Wolfgang Müller von Königswinter (*Gedichte* [Frankfurt, 1847], 158–60) three hundred years; Johannes Herolt (*Sermones discipuli de tempore,* sermo 84), three hundred and fifty years; and Martin of Poland (*Promptuarium,* chap. 16) three hundred and sixty-five years. In the Longfellow's poem "A Farm in the Odenwald" (*The Golden Legend,* II, 1) about the monk Felix, it is described as one hundred years.
2. Biblioteka Uniwersytecka we Wrocławiu, ms. I. F. 115.
3. Motif F1: *Journey to otherworld as dream or vision.*
4. Motif E 721: *Soul journeys from the body.*
5. Motif E 755.2.7: *Devils torment sinners in hell.*
6. Motif V 232: *Angel as helper.*
7. Motif V 238: *Guardian angel.*
8. Motif Q 560: *Punishments in hell.*
9. Motif F 759.2: *Hollow mountain.*
10. Cf. motif F 152: *Bridge to otherworld.*
11. Motif F 531: *Giant.*
12. Line 273 of the Middle High German text in Palmer, ed., *Tondolus der Ritter,* 55. This name is most likely a corruption of Acharon (i.e., Acheron, a river in Hades) and Cherberus (i.e., Cerberus, the "hound of Hades") from Greek mythology.

13. In fact, the two Irish kings cited are Fergus mac Róich and Conall Cernach, according to the Latin text of Brother Marcus (1148); cf. Seymour, "Studies in the Vision of Tundal."
14. The distinction between *sacrilegium regale* (local) and *sacrilegium personale* is evident. Gratian's *Decretum* defines sacrilege as follows: "Sacrilegium ergo est, quotiens quis sacrum violat, uel auferendo sacrum de sacro, uel sacrum de non sacro, uel non sacrum de sacro" (Friedberg, ed., *Corpus Iuris Canonici*, vol. I., col. 820).
15. A version of Psalm 84:11 [Vulgate].
16. Motifs D 661: *Transformation as punishment*; D 191: *Transformation: man to serpent (snake).*
17. Behind this entire description is a recollection of the *Physiologus,* the most widespread bestiary of the Middle Ages. The chapter on the viper informs us that its young emerge from its mother by ripping her body open from the inside. This is all based on an etymological interpretation of *vipera* as *vivipera* (*vivi parere* [from *vivus* "alive" + *parere* "to bring forth"]); the passage that seems to have been the inspiration for our author is: "cum autem creverint catuli in ventre, viperam perforant mordentes latus eius, et sic exeunt mortua matre."
18. Motif E 80: *Water of life.*
19. Cf. Psalm 127:2 [Vulgate].
20. Cf. motif F 148: *Wall around otherworld.*
21. Cf. Psalm 120:8 [Vulgate].
22. Motif V 522: *Sinner reformed after visit to heaven and hell.*
23. Psalm 106:13 [Vulgate].
24. Reversal of Motif F 342.1: *Fairies give coals (wood, earth) that turns to gold.*
25. Cf. John 8:44.

3. TRAVELS IN THE LAND OF FAERY

1. Motif F 252.2: *Fairy queen.*
2. *Þou gyffe me leue to lye the bye!* (l. 100).
3. Motif F 211: *Fairyland under hollow knoll, usually entered under the roots of trees.*
4. *Whare it was dirke als mydnyght myrke* (l. 171).
5. Motif F 141.1: *River as barrier to otherworld.*
6. This phrase comes from another manuscript transcribed by Sir Walter Scott in *Minstrelsy of the Scottish Border,* vol. 2, 262–321: "and they waded

through red blude to the knee; / For a' the blude that's shed on earth / Rins through the springs o' that countrie"; another version can be found in Child, *English and Scottish Popular Ballads,* 63–66.

7. *Thi saule gose to þe fyre of helle* (l. 190).
8. Motif C 401: *Taboo: speaking during certain time.*
9. Motif F 377: *Supernatural lapse of time in fairyland.*
10. Motif F 340: *Gifts from fairies.*
11. Clifton-Everest, *The Tragedy of Knighthood,* 136–43.
12. Sale, *Le Paradis de la reine Sibylle*; Mora, *Antoine de la Sale: Voyages en Sibyllie.*
13. Motif F 131.1: *Mountain of Venus: Hollow mountain otherworld where men live a life of ease and lustful pleasure in company with beautiful women.*
14. Variant of Motif Q 521.1.1: *Penance: crawling on knees and watering a dry staff until it blooms.*
15. Facsimile in Könnecke, *Bilderatlas zur Geschichte der deutschen Nationalliteratur,* 124.
16. Cf. the story type AT 756: *The hard penance and the green twigs on the dry branch.*
17. One example: *Guerino detto il Meschino: Storia in cui si tratta delle grandi imprese e vittorie da lui riportate contro i Turchi* (Milan: A spese degli Editori, 1841).
18. *Le Premier livre de Guerin Mesquin* (Lyon: Arnoullet, 1530).
19. *Cy commance l'Histoire du premier livre de Guerin Mesquin, fils de Millon de Bourgongne,* etc. (Troyes: Oudot, 1628). I would like to thank Marie-Dominique Leclerc, who provided me with reproductions of the text, and Stefano Mangano for his help with the translation of certain passages from the Italian text.
20. Motif B 42: *Griffin.*
21. Psalm 70 (69), 1 [Vulgate].
22. Motif P 426.2: *Hermit.*
23. Motif F 141.1: *River as barrier to otherworld.*
24. Motif F 91: *Door entrance to lower world.*
25. Motif F 162.1: *Garden in otherworld.*
26. Cf. motif M 110.3: *Oath uttered by pious when in danger of succumbing to temptation.*
27. The entire passage in italics does not exist in the Venice version. It appears in that of 1758 in which the fairy is likened to the Sibilla Appenninica (Sibyl of the Apennines), if not identified with her.

28. Motif C 200: *Taboo: eating.*
29. Motif D 620: *Periodic transformation.*
30. Motifs D 199.2: *Transformation: man to dragon*; D 661: *Transformation as punishment.*
31. In *Les Livres dou Trésor* (II, 6), Brunetto Latini (ca. 1220–1294) writes: "La ame de l'home a.iii. Poissances : l'une est vegetative, et ce est comun as arbres et as plantes, car il ont ame vegetative aussi con li home ont; la seconde est apelee sensitive, et c'est comun a totes bestes, car eles ont ame sensitive; la tierce est apelee raisonable, por ce est li hom divers de toutes choses, por ce que nule autre chose n'a ame raisonable se l'ome non" (Man's soul has three potencies: one is vegetative, and is as common to trees and plants, for they possess a vegetative soul just as man; the second is called sensitive, and is common to all beasts, for they have a sensitive soul; the third is called reasonable, because it is of the man varied in all things, and that no other thing has a reasonable soul).
32. Motif Z 71.5.6.2: *Seven deadly sins.*
33. A reference to the *Aeneid* of Virgil.
34. "Ô inique et peruerse faee mauldite de dieu eternal" (Jean de Rochemeure).
35. "Je ne suis pas corps fantastique" (Jean de Rochemeure).
36. The French chapbook version has: "J'ai esperance en dieu de trouver plutost mon pere au monde qu'aux enfers" (I place my hope in God that I find my father in heaven rather than hell).
37. The French chapbook has: "Nul amour n'est en nous et ne sera" (No love is within us and nor will there ever be).
38. The French chapbook has: "une ville femme pleine d'iniquité" (an old woman full of sin).
39. His battle against Astiladoro and the Turks is recounted in bk. II, chap. 33ff.
40. Cf. bk. II, chap. 60–62, which distinguishes it from the legend of Alexander the Great. In the French chapbook, the trees announce: "You have the name of Guerrin & have been baptized two times & you are the son of a Christian baron: you are an extraction of royal blood."
41. Barberino, *Guerino detto il Meschino* (Venice: Baroni, 1689).

4. DUKE ERNST

1. For the original text of the lay, see King, ed., *Das Lied von Herzog Ernst.*
2. Ll. 1–2122.

3. Motif F 771.4.3: *Abandoned castle.*
4. The German text is quite obscure here; I am using the *Gesta Ernesti ducis* (l. 1220), the Latin translation, in which we read: *Augustissimum palacium rotundum, quod vulgo wrmlage dicitur, ibi habebatur* (ll. 90–92). The semantic field of "*wrmlage*" (= Middle High German *würmelage,* "serpent enclosure") is quite vast; cf. Jacobsen and Orth, eds., *Gesta Ernesti ducis,* 12–24.
5. The bed and bed linen are the subject of a long description (ll. 2590–645).
6. Cf. Lecouteux, "À propos d'un épisode de *Herzog Ernst*: la rencontre des hommes-grues"; likewise, Lecouteux, "Die Kranichschnäbler der *Herzog Ernst*-Dichtung."
7. Motif F 754: *Magnetic mountain. Pulls nails out of ships that approach it.*
8. For more on this legend, cf. Lecouteux, *Les Monstres dans la littérature allemande du Moyen Âge,* 633–34. The griffin corresponds to a bird called the roc, found in Middle Eastern literature. In the tales of *The One Thousand and One Nights*, it is said that it can carry off an elephant.
9. The Old French *Romance of Alexander* (*Roman d'Alexandre,* ed. Armstrong) provides a similar story concerning Alexander the Great: He has set sail in a flimsy vessel and is surprised by a storm at sea. He kills a chicken that he had brought with him and smears its blood over a lion hide. He then fashions a sack from the hide and slips inside of it. The griffins seize what they mistake for a ham and carry the Macedonian to the island of Orion (ll. 7602–614). See also Caldarini, "Fantasie e 'mirabilia' nel 'Roman d'Alexandre.'"
10. Cf. motif D 1520.5.4: *Magic transportation by horseskin.*
11. Benjamin of Tudela, *The Itinerary*, 143–44 (archaicisms and punctuation modernized).

5. SOLOMON AND MARCOLF

1. Motif R 10: *Abduction.*
2. Motif D 1076: *Magic ring.*
3. Motif D 965: *Magic plant.*
4. Motif H 248: *Test of death: to see whether person is dead or feigning.*
5. Motif K 1821: *Disguise by changing bodily appearance.*
6. Motif F 679.8: *Skill at chess-playing.*
7. Motif D 1620: *Magic automata.*

8. Motif K 625: *Escape by giving narcotic to guards.*
9. Motif K 625.2: *Escape by making the watchmen drunk.*
10. Motif K 1817.2: *Disguise as palmer (pilgrim).*
11. Cf. motif D 1421.5.1: *Magic horn summons army for rescue.*
12. Motif K 1818: *Disguise as sick man.*
13. Motif K 1817.3: *Disguise as harper (minstrel).*
14. Motif P 448: *Butcher.*
15. Motif F 420.1.2: *Water-spirit as woman (water-nymph, water-nix).*
16. Motif F 451: *Dwarf.*

7. ŠTILFRÍD AND BRUNCVÍK

1. Cf. Lecouteux and Lecouteux, *Contes, diableries et autres merveilles du Moyen Âge*, 174–84.
2. *Povídka o Bruncvíkovi*; *Kroniky dvě o Štilfrídovi a Bruncvíkovi*; *Kronika o Štilfrídovi a Bruncvíkovi*; *Kronika o Bruncvíkovi*; *Dvě kroniky o Štilfrídovi a Bruncvíkovi.*
3. *Сказание о кралевиче Брунцвике ческие земли* (Skazanie o kraleviče Bruncvíke českie zemli).
4. Motif F 754: *Magnetic mountain*; cf. Lecouteux, "La Montagne d'Aimant."
5. A siren. Motif B 53: *Siren*; cf. Lecouteux, "La sirène dans l'Antiquité classique et au Moyen Âge."
6. Motif B 42: *Griffin.*
7. Motif B 11.2.3: *Many-headed dragon.*
8. Cf. Taloş, *Omul şi leul*; for more on dragons, see Lecouteux, "Der Drache."
9. Variant of Motif B 381: *Thorn removed from lion's paw (Androcles and the Lion). In gratitude the lion later rewards the man.*
10. On the isles, cf. Lecouteux, "La mer et ses îles au Moyen Âge."
11. Motif G 301: *Monsters.*
12. Motif B 25.1.2: *Dog-headed people.* In addition to the easily identified human monsters, the Monopodes, also known as Skiapodes (σκιαποδες), and the Cynocephali (κυνοκέφαλοi) are mentioned here. These latter can also be found in Arab literature; cf. Ansbacher, *Die Abschnitte über die Geister und wunderbaren Geschöpfe aus Qazwînî's Kosmographie,* 31.
13. This gate is borrowed from the legend of the enclosing of the monstrous being Gog and Magog in front of the gates of the Caucasus, a legend transmitted by Josephus, *The Jewish War,* I, 6, 1 and VII, 7, 4; the *Apocalypse*

of Pseudo-Methodius (cf. appendix); and the Old French *Romance of Alexander,* cf. Pfister, *Kleine Schriften zum Alexanderroman,* 175–76.

14. Motifs B 510: *Healing by animals*; D 1500.1.4: *Magic healing plant.*
15. Motif D 1081: *Magic sword.*

BY WAY OF CONCLUSION. THE PRIEST AMIS, AN ADVENTURER

1. Kamihara, ed., *Des Strickers Pfaffe Amis.*
2. Cf. Blume and Wunderlich, eds., *Hermen Bote.*
3. Bote, *Ein kurtzweilig lesen von Dil Ulenspiegel, geboren vß dem land zu Brunßwick, wie er sein leben volbracht hat. xcvi seiner geschichten* (1515); *Ein kurtzweilig Lesen von Dil Ulenspiegel, nach dem Druck von 1515 mit 87 Holzschnitten,* ed. Lindow. Till Eulenspiegel is a historical figure who died in 1350.
4. Manuel, *Libro del conde Lucanor,* ed. Redondo.
5. Motif K 1870: *Illusions.*
6. Motif J 2312: *Naked person made to believe that he is clothed.*
7. Motif K1 825.1: *Disguise as doctor.*
8. Cf. motif K 1955.1: *Sham physician cures people by threatening them with death.*

Bibliography

Aarne, Antti. *The Types of the Folktale: A Classification and a Bibliography*. Translated and enlarged by Stith Thompson. Second revised edition. Helsinki: Suomalainen Tiedeakatemia, 1964.

Adam of Bremen. *Gesta Hammaburgensis Ecclesiae Pontificum*. English edition: *History of the Archbishops of Hamburg-Bremen*. Translated by Francis J. Tschan. New York: Columbia University Press, 1959.

Ansbacher, Jonas. *Die Abschnitte über die Geister und wunderbaren Geschöpfe aus Qazwînî's Kosmographie*. Kirchhain N.-L.: Schmersow, 1905.

Augustine. *De Genesi ad litteram*. In Augustine, *Œuvres,* vol. 48. Edited by Aimé Solignac and Pierre Agaësse. Paris: Brouwer, 1972.

Babbi, Anna Maria. "Le traduzioni del *Guerrin Meschino* in Francia." In *Il romanzo nella Francia del Rinascimento: dall'eredità medievale all'Astrea,* 133–41. Fasano: Schena, 1996.

———. "Le *Guerrin Meschino* d'Andrea da Barberino et le remaniement de Jean de Rochemeure." *Le Moyen français* 51–52–53 (2003): 9–18.

———. "Jean de Rochemeure, traduttore del *Guerrin Meschino*." In *Filologia romanza e cultura medievale: Studi in onore di Elio Melli*. Edited by A. Fassò, L. Formisano, and M. Mancini, 15–23.. Alessandria: dell'Orso, 1998.

Barberino, Andrea de' Magnabotti da. *Cy commance l'Histoire du premier livre de Guerin Mesquin, fils de Millon de Bourgongne,* etc. Translated by Jean Decuchermoys [Jean de Rochemeure]. Troyes: Oudot, 1628.

———. *Guerino detto il Meschino. Nel quale si tratta, come trouó suo Padre, & sua Madre nella città di Durazzo in prigione et diuerse Vittorie hauute contra Turchi*. Venice: Baroni, 1689.

———. *Guerino detto il Meschino: Storia in cui si trata delle grandi imprese e vittorie da lui riportate contro i Turchi*. Revised and illustrated, with notes by Giuseppe Berta. Milan: spese degli Editori, 1841.

———. *Le Premier livre de Guerin Mesquin*. Translated by Jehan Decuchermoys [Jean de Rochemeure]. Lyon: Arnoullet, 1530.

Bartsch, Karl, ed. *Herzog Ernst*. Vienna: Braumüller, 1869.

Baumann, Winfried. *Die Sage von Heinrich dem Löwen bei den Slaven*. Munich: Sagner, 1975.

Benjamin of Tudela. *The Itinerary of Rabbi Benjamin of Tudela*, vol. 1. Translated and edited by A. Asher. New York: Hakesheth, 1900.

Bergmeister, Hermann-Josef. *Die historia de preliis Alexandri Magni (Der lateinische Alexanderroman des Mittelalters). Synoptische Edition der Rezensionen des Leo Archipresbyter und der interpolierten Fassungen J1, J2, J3 (Buch I und II)*. Meisenheim am Glan: Hain, 1975.

Blume, Herbert, and Werner Wunderlich, eds. *Hermen Bote: Bilanz und Perspektive der Forschung*. Göppingen: Kümmerle, 1982.

Bote, Hermann. *Ein kurtzweilig lesen von Dil Ulenspiegel, geboren vß dem land zu Brunßwick, wie er sein leben volbracht hat. xcvi seiner geschichten*. Strasbourg: Grüninger, 1515.

———. *Ein kurtzweilig Lesen von Dil Ulenspiegel, nach dem Druck von 1515 mit 87 Holzschnitten*. Edited by Wolfgang Lindow. Stuttgart, 1966.

Budge, E. A. Wallis. *The Life and Exploits of Alexander the Great, Being a Series of Translations of the Ethiopic Histories of Alexander by the Pseudo-Callisthenes and Other Writers*. London: Clay & Sons, 1896.

Burkhart, F. *Die äthiopische Alexanderlegende, eingeleitet, nach 2 Hss. herausgegeben und übersetzt*. Dissertation, Charles University, Prague, 1942.

Caldarini, Ernesta. "Fantasie e 'mirabilia' nel 'Roman d'Alexandre.'" *Studi di Letteratura Francese* 13 (1987): 17–29.

Černá, Alena M. *Povídka o Bruncvíkovi, text Baworowský*. Prague: Ústav pro jazyk český, 2009.

Child, Francis. *English and Scottish Popular Ballads*. Edited by Helen Child Sargent & George Lyman Kittredge. Boston and New York: Houghton Mifflin, 1904.

Christians, Dagmar. *Die serbische Alexandreis nach der Sofioter illustrierten Handschrift Nr. 771*. Vienna and Cologne: Böhlau, 1991.

Clifton-Everest, J. M. *The Tragedy of Knighthood: Origins of the Tannhäuser-legend*. Oxford: Society for the Study of Mediæval Languages and Literature, 1979.

Curschmann, Michael. *"Spielmannsepik": Wege und Ergebnisse der Forschung von 1907–1965*. Stuttgart: Metzler, 1968.

Delarue, Paul, and Marie-Louise Ténèze. *Le Conte populaire français.* 4 vols. Paris: Maisonneuve et Larose, 2002.

Donath, L. *Die Alexandersage in Talmud und Midrasch, mit Rücksicht auf Josephus Flavius, Pseudo-Callisthenes und die mohammedanische Alexandersage.* Dissertation, University of Rostock, 1873.

Dvě kroniky o knížatech českých, první o Stylfrydovi, druhá o Bruncvíkovi. Olmütz [Olomouc]: Günther, 1568.

Ehlen, Thomas, ed. *Hystoria ducis Bauarie Ernesti: Kritische Edition des "Herzog Ernst" C und Untersuchungen zu Struktur und Darstellung des Stoffes in den volkssprachlichen und lateinischen Fassungen.* Tübingen: Narr, 1996.

Enzyklopädie des Märchens. Edited by Kurt Ranke, et al. 11 vols. Berlin and New York: De Gruyter, 1979–2006.

Erben, Karel Jaromír, ed. *Výbor z literatury české,* vol. II. Prague: Museum království cěského, 1868.

Ethé, C. H. "Alexanders Zug zum Lebensquell im Land der Finsternis." *Sitzungsberichte der Bayerischen Akademie der Wissenschaften: Philosophisch-Historische Klasse* (1871): 343–405.

Fahd, Toufic. "Anges, démons et djinns en Islam." In *Génies, anges et démons,* edited by Denise Bernot, 153–215. Paris: Seuil, 1971.

Feldbusch, Michael, ed. *Der Brief Alexanders an Aristoteles über die Wunder Indiens.* Synoptic edition. Meisenheim am Glan: Hain, 1976.

Friedberg, Emil, ed. *Corpus Iuris Canonici,* vol. I. Leipzig: Tauchnitz, 1879.

Friedlaender, Israel. *Die Chadhirlegende und der Alexanderroman: Eine sagengeschichtliche und literarhistorische Untersuchung.* Leipzig and Berlin: Teubner, 1913.

Flood, John L., ed. *Die Historie von Herzog Ernst: Die Frankfurter Prosafassung des 16. Jahrhunderts.* Berlin: Schmidt, 1992.

Gansweidt, Birgit, ed. *Der "Ernestus" des Odo von Magdeburg: Kritische Edition mit Kommentar eines lateinischen Epos aus dem 13. Jahrhundert.* Munich: Arbeo-Gesellschaft, 1989.

Gaudé, Laurent. *La Porte des enfers.* Paris: Actes Sud, 2008.

Grimm, Jacob, and Wilhelm Grimm. *Deutsche Sagen.* Edited by Heinz Rölleke. Frankfurt: Deutscher Klassiker, 1994.

Hammerich, Louis Leonor. *Munken og fuglen: en middelalderstudie.* Copenhagen: Lunos, 1933.

Haupt, Barbara. "*Der Pfaffe Amis* und *Ulenspiegel*: Variationen zu einem vorgegebenen Thema." In *Till Eulenspiegel in Geschichte und Gegenwart.* Edited by Thomas Cramer. Bern: Lang, 1978.

Heidlauf, Felix, ed. *Lucidarius, aus der Berliner Handschrift.* Berlin: Weidmann, 1915.

Herodotus. *The History* [= *Histories*]. Translated by David Greene. Chicago and London: University of Chicago Press, 1987.

Hilka, Alfons, ed. *Der altfranzösische Prosa-Alexanderroman nach der Berliner Bilderhandschrift nebst dem lateinischen Original der Historia de preliis (Rezension J²).* Halle: Niemeyer, 1922. Reprinted Geneva: Slatkine, 1974.

———, ed. *Historia Alexandri Magni (Historia de preliis) Rezension J² (Orosius-Rezension),* 2 vols. Meisenheim am Glan: Hain, 1976–1977.

Jacobsen, Peter Christian, and Peter Orth, eds. *Gesta Ernesti ducis: Die Erfurter Prosa-Fassung der Sage von den Kämpfen und Abenteuern des Herzog Ernst.* Erlangen: Universitätsbund Erlangen-Nürnberg, 1997.

Jacoby, Felix. *Fragmente der griechischen Historiker.* Berlin: Weidmann, 1923.

Josephus. *The Jewish War.* With an English translation by H. St. J. Thackeray. 2 vols. London: Heinemann, 1927–28.

Kamihara, Kin'ichi, ed. *Des Strickers Pfaffe Amis.* Göppingen: Kümmerle, 1978.

Kaplowitt, Stephen J. "The Heathens in Salman und Morolf." *Archiv für das Studium der neueren Sprachen und Literaturen* 213 (1976): 95–99.

Kappler, Claire. "Métamorphoses alchimiques de la mort en littérature persane classique: Key Khosrow, Alexandre le Grande et Bahrâm Gûr." In *Alchimies Occident-Orient,* edited Claire Kappler and Suzanne Thiolier-Méjean, 249–79. Paris: L'Harmattan, 2006.

Karnein, Alfred, ed. *Salman und Morolf.* Tübingen: Niemeyer, 1979.

King, K. C., ed. *Das Lied von Herzog Ernst.* Berlin: Schmidt, 1959.

Könnecke, Gustav. *Bilderatlas zur Geschichte der deutschen Nationalliteratur.* 2nd edition. Marburg: Elwert, 1912.

Könneker, Barbara. "Strickers Pfaffe Amis und das Volksbuch von Ulenspiegel." *Euphorion* 64 (1970): 242–80.

Laing, David, ed. *Select Remains of the Ancient Popular Poetry of Scotland.* Revised by John Small. Edinburgh: Blackwood and Sons, 1885.

Latini, Brunetto. *Les Livres dou trésor.* Edited by Francis Carmody. Berkeley and Los Angeles: University of California Press, 1948.

Lecouteux Claude. "À propos d'un épisode de *Herzog Ernst*: la rencontre des hommes-grues." *Études germaniques* 33 (1978): 1–15.

———. "Der Drache." *Zeitschrift für deutsches Altertum* 108 (1979): 13–31.

———. "Die Kranichschnäbler der *Herzog Ernst*-Dichtung." *Euphorion* 75 (1981): 100–102.

———. *Kleine Texte zur Alexandersage, mit einem Anhang: Prestre Jean.* Göppingen, Kümmerle, 1984 (G.A.G. n° 388).

———. "La mer et ses îles au Moyen Âge: Un voyage dans le merveilleux." In *Démons et Merveilles: Le surnaturel dans l'Océan Indien.* Edited by Valérie Magdeleine-Andrianjafitrimo, et al., 11–24. Sainte-André: Océan, 2005.

———. *Mondes parallèles, l'univers des croyances au Moyen Âge,* 2nd edition. Paris: Champion, 2007.

———. *Les Monstres dans la littérature allemande du Moyen Âge: Contribution à l'étude du merveilleux médiéval.* Besançon: Éditions la Völva, 2016.

———. "La Montagne d'Aimant." In *La Montagne dans le texte médiéval: Entre mythe et réalité.* Edited by Claude Thomasset and Danièle James-Raoul, 167–86. Paris: PUPS, 2000.

———. "La sirène dans l'Antiquité classique et au Moyen Âge." In *Les Filles des eaux dans l'Océan indien: Mythes, récits, représentations.* Edited by Bernard Terramorsi, 27–51. Paris: L'Harmattan, 2010.

———. "Zur Vermittlung mittelalterlicher sagenhafter Erzählstoffe: Die Glossare und Lexika als paraliterarischer Weg." *Chloe* 16 (1993): 19–35.

Lecouteux, Corinne, and Claude Lecouteux. *Contes, diableries et autres merveilles du Moyen Âge.* Paris: Imago, 2015.

Lexikon des Mittelalters, vol. 1. Munich & Zurich: Artemis, 1978.

Lévi, Israel. "La légende d'Alexandre dans le Talmud." *Revue des études juives* 2 (1881): 293–300.

———. "La légende d'Alexandre dans le Talmud et le Midrasch." *Revue des études juives* 7 (1883): 78–93.

Lidzbarski, Mark. "Wer ist Chadhir?" *Zeitschrift für Assyriologie* 7 (1892): 104–116.

Löhmann, Otto. "Die Entstehung der Tannhäusersage." *Fabula* 3 (1960): 224–53.

Manuel, Don Juan. *Libro del conde Lucanor.* Edited by Fernando Gómez Redondo. Madrid: Castalia, 1987.

Meier, John, ed., *Deutsche Volkslieder mit ihren Melodien*. Berlin: De Gruyter, 1935.

Meusel, Heinrich, ed. *Pseudo-Callisthenes nach der Leidener Handschrift herausgegeben*. Leipzig: Teubner, 1871.

Micha, Alexandre. *Voyages dans l'au-delà: D'après des textes médiévaux (IVe–XIIIe siècles)*. Paris: Klincksieck, 1992.

Montorsi, Francesco. "*Le Guérin Mesquin,* traduit par Jehan de Cucharmois, natif de Lyon." *Réforme, Humanisme, Renaissance* 71/1 (2011): 73–89.

Müller, Fritz. *Die Legende vom verzückten Mönch, den ein Vöglein in das Paradies leitet*. Dissertation, Erlangen, 1912.

Murray, James A. H., ed. *The Romance and Prophecies of Thomas of Erceldoune: Printed from Five Manuscripts with Illustrations from the Prophetic Literature of the 15th and 16th Centuries*. London: Trübner, 1875.

Mora, Francine, ed. *Antoine de la Sale: Voyages en Sibyllie. Les hommes, le paradis et l'enfer*. Paris: Riveneuve, 2010.

Otloh von St. Emmeram. *Liber Visionum*. Edited by Paul Gerhard Schmidt. Weimar: Böhlau, 1989.

Palmer, Nigel F., ed. *Tondolus der Ritter: Die von J. und C. Hist gedruckte Fassung*. Munich: Fink, 1980.

———. *"Visio Tnugdali": The German and Dutch Translations and Their Circulation in the Later Middle Ages*. Munich & Zurich: Artemis, 1982.

Paudler, Fritz. *Die Volkserzählungen von der Abschaffung der Altentötung*. Helsinki: Suomalainen Tiedeakatemia, 1937.

Petrovskij, M., ed. *История о славном короле Брунцвике*. St. Petersburg, 1888.

Pfister, Friedrich. *Kleine Schriften zum Alexanderroman*. Meisenheim am Glan: Hain, 1976.

Pliny. *Natural History* [= *Historia naturalis*]. 10 volumes. Cambridge, Mass.: Harvard University Press, 1961–68.

Polczynska, Edyta. *Studien zum "Salman und Morolf."* Poznan: UAM, 1968.

Polivká, Jiří. *Kronika o Bruncvíkovi v ruské literatuře*. Prague: Nákl. České akademie Císaře Františka Josefa pro vědy, slovesnost a umění, 1892.

Pseudo-Methodius. *Apocalypse*. In: *Apocalypse Pseudo-Methodius / An Alexandrian World Chronicle*. Edited and translated by Benjamin Garstad. Cambridge, Mass: Harvard University Press, 2012.

Raabe, Richard, ed. *ιστορία Αλεξάνδρου: Die armenische Übersetzung der sagenhaften Alexanderbiographie (Pseudo-Callisthenes)*. Leipzig: Hinrichs, 1896.

Ribbeck, Konrad. *Danuser, eine alte niederdeutsche Fassung des Tannhäuser-liedes nach einer Handschrift des Essener Stadtarchivs.* Essen: Fredebeul & Koenen, 1926.

Robson, C. A. *Maurice of Sully and the Medieval Vernacular Homily with the Text of Maurice's French Homilies from a Sens Cathedral Chapter ms.* Oxford: Blackwell, 1952.

Röhrich, Lutz. *Erzählungen des späten Mittelalters und ihr Weiterleben in Literatur und Volksdichtung bis zur Gegenwart,* vol. 1. Bern & Munich: Francke, 1962.

Ryssel, Viktor. "Die syrische Übersetzung des Pseudo-Kallisthenes." *Archiv für das Studium der neueren Sprachen und Literaturen* 90 (1893): 83–134; 269–88; 353–402.

[*Roman d'Alexandre*] *The Medieval French Roman d'Alexandre.* Edited by E. C. Armstrong. 7 vols. Princeton, N.J.: Princeton University Press, 1937–76.

Sale, Antoine de la. *Le Paradis de la reine Sibylle.* Edited by F. Desonay. Paris: Droz, 1930.

Sárdi, Margit S. "Von Braunschweig bis Bruncvik: Volksbuch und Volksmärchen." In *Fortunatus, Melusine, Genovefa: Internationale Erzählstoffe in der deutschen und ungarischen Literatur der Frühen Neuzeit,* edited by Dieter Breuer & Gábor Tüskés, 377–418. Bern and Berlin: Lang, 2010.

Scherf, Walter. *Das Märchenlexikon.* 2 vols. Munich: Beck, 1995.

Schröder, Walter Johannes. *Spielmannsepik.* Darmstadt: Wissenschaftliche Buchgesellschaft, 1977.

Scott, Walter. *Minstrelsy of the Scottish Border.* Vol. 2. Edinburgh: Longman & Rees, 1803.

Settis-Frugoni, Chiara. *Historia Alexandri elevati per griphos ad aerem (origine, iconografia e fortuna di un tema).* Rome: Istituto storico italiano per il Medio Evo, 1973.

Seymour, St. J. D. "Studies in the Vision of Tundal." *Proceedings of the Royal Irish Academy* 37 C, 4 (1925): 87–106.

Solinus. *Collectanea rerum memorabilium.* Edited by Theodor Mommsen. Berlin: Weidmann, 1895.

Stoneman, Richard. *Legends of Alexander the Great.* London and New York: Tauris, 2012.

Taloş, Ion. *Omul şi leul: Studiu de antropologi culturală.* Bucharest: Academiei Române, 2013.

Thompson, Stith. *Motif-Index of Folk-Literature: A Classification of Narrative*

Elements in Folk-Tales, Ballads, Myths, Fables, Mediaeval Romances, Exempla, Fabliaux, Jest-Books, and Local Legends. Revised and enlarged edition. 6 vols. Copenhagen: Rosenkilde and Bagger, 1955–1958.

Tondolus der Ritter. Speyer: Hist, n.d. [ca. 1495].

Tubach, Frederic C. *Index Exemplorum: A Handbook of Medieval Religious Tales.* Helsinki: Suomalainen Tiedeakatemia, 1969.

Ueltschi, Karin. "Sibylle, Arthur et Sainte Agathe: les monts italiens comme carrefour des autres mondes." In *Materiali arturiani nelle letterature di Provenza, Spagna, Italia.* Edited by Margherita Lecco, 142–64. Alessandria: dell' Orso, 2006.

Voborník, Jan, ed. *Dvě kroniky o Štilfrídovi a Bruncvíkovi.* Prague: Brož, 1918.

Wagner, Albrecht, ed. *Visio Tnugdali lateinisch und altdeutsch.* Erlangen: Deichert, 1882.

Wenzel, Siegfried. *The Sin of Sloth: Acedia in Medieval Thought and Literature.* Chapel Hill: University of North Carolina Press, 1967.

Werber, Bernard. *Les Thanatonautes.* Paris: Michel, 1994.

Weymann, Karl Friedrich. *Die äthiopischen und arabischen Übersetzungen des Pseudo-Kallisthenes.* Kirchhain: Zahn & Baendel, 1901.

Wünsche, August. "Alexanders Zug nach dem Lebensquell: Eine Episode aus dem Alexanderroman." *Jahrbuch für jüdische Geschichte und Literatur* 1 (1898): 109–131.

Folk Motifs in the Tales and Legends

ALEXANDER'S LETTER TO OLYMPIAS

A 692: *Islands of the blest.*

B 552: *Man carried by bird.*

D 199.3: *Transformation: woman to siren.*

D 95: *Transformation: man to demon.*

F 511.0.1: *Headless person.*

F 531: *Giant.*

F 706: *Land of darkness.*

G 11.2: *Cannibal giant.*

H 1376.7: *Quest for immortality.*

N 825.2: *Old man helper.*

V 230: *Angels.*

DHUL-QARNAYN'S ENTRY INTO DARKNESS

E 80: *Water of life.*

F 403.2.2.2: *Angels as familiar spirits.*

F 706: *Land of darkness.*

ALEXANDER'S LETTER TO ARISTOTLE

D 1610.2: *Speaking tree.*

THE PRINCE IN PARADISE

F 377.1: *Supernatural lapse of time in paradise.*

TUNDALE THE KNIGHT

D 191: *Transformation: man to serpent (snake).*
D 661: *Transformation as punishment.*
E 721: *Soul journeys from the body.*
E 755.2.7: *Devils torment sinners in hell.*
E 80: *Water of life.*
F 148: *Wall around otherworld.*
F 152: *Bridge to otherworld.*
F 531: *Giant.*
F 759.2: *Hollow mountain.*
F1: *Journey to otherworld as dream or vision.*
Q 560: *Punishments in hell.*
V 232: *Angel as helper.*
V 238: *Guardian angel.*
V 522: *Sinner reformed after visit to heaven and hell.*

GUESTS OF THE DEVIL

F 342.1: *Fairies give coals (wood, earth) that turns to gold* (reversal of the motif).

THOMAS OF ERCELDOUNE

C 401: *Taboo: speaking during certain time.*

F 141.1: *River as barrier to otherworld.*

F 211: *Fairyland under hollow knoll, usually entered under the roots of trees.*

F 252.2: *Fairy queen.*

F 340: *Gifts from fairies.*

F 377: *Supernatural lapse of time in fairyland.*

THE SONG OF TANNHÄUSER

F 131.1: *Mountain of Venus. Hollow mountain otherworld where men live a life of ease and lustful pleasure in company with beautiful women.*

Q 521.1.1: *Penance: crawling on knees and watering a dry staff until it blooms.*

GUERRIN MESCHINO AT THE HOME OF THE FAIRY ALCINA

B 42: *Griffin.*

C 200: *Taboo: Eating.*

D 199.2: *Transformation: man to dragon.*

D 620: *Periodic transformation.*

D 661: *Transformation as punishment.*

D 191: *Transformation: man to serpent.*

F 141.1: *River as barrier to otherworld.*

F 162.1: *Garden in otherworld.*

F 91: *Door entrance to lower world.*

M 110.3: *Oath uttered by pious when in danger of succumbing to temptation.*

P 426.2: *Hermit.*

Z 71.5.6.2: *Seven deadly sins.*

DUKE ERNST

D 1520.5.4: *Magic transportation by horseskin.*

F 754: *Magnetic mountain. Pulls nails out of ships that approach it.*

F 771.4.3: *Abandoned castle.*

SOLOMON AND MARCOLF

D 1076: *Magic ring.*

D 1421.5.1: *Magic horn summons army for rescue.*

D 1620: *Magic automata.*

D 965: *Magic plant.*

F 420.1.2: *Water-spirit as woman (water-nymph, water-nix).*

F 451: *Dwarf.*

F 679.8: *Skill at chess-playing.*

H 248: *Test of death: to see whether person is dead or feigning.*

K 1817.2: *Disguise as palmer (pilgrim).*

K 1817.3: *Disguise as harper (minstrel).*

K 1818: *Disguise as sick man.*

K 1821: *Disguise by changing bodily appearance.*

K 625: *Escape by giving narcotic to guards.*

K 625.2: *Escape by making the watchmen drunk.*

P 448: *Butcher.*

R 10: *Abduction.*

ŠTILFRÍD AND BRUNCVÍK

B 11.2.3: *Many-headed dragon.*

B 25.1.2: *Dog-headed people.*

B 381: *Androcles and the lion. In gratitude the lion later rewards the man* (variant).

B 42: *Griffin.*

B 510: *Healing by animals.*

B 53: *Siren.*

D 1081: *Magic sword.*

D 1500.1.4: *Magic healing plant.*

F 754: *Magnetic mountain.*

G 301: *Monsters.*

THE PRIEST AMIS, AN ADVENTURER

J 2312: *Naked person made to believe that he is clothed.*

K 1870: *Illusions.*

K 1955.1: *Sham physician cures people by threatening them with death* (variant).

K1 825.1: *Disguise as doctor.*

Index

Page numbers in *italics* indicate illustrations.

BOOKS OF RELATED INTEREST

The Hidden History of Elves and Dwarfs
Avatars of Invisible Realms
by Claude Lecouteux

Dictionary of Gypsy Mythology
Charms, Rites, and Magical Traditions of the Roma
by Claude Lecouteux

Traditional Magic Spells for Protection and Healing
by Claude Lecouteux

Encyclopedia of Norse and Germanic Folklore, Mythology, and Magic
by Claude Lecouteux

Dictionary of Ancient Magic Words and Spells
From Abraxas to Zoar
by Claude Lecouteux

The Tradition of Household Spirits
Ancestral Lore and Practices
by Claude Lecouteux

The Book of Grimoires
The Secret Grammar of Magic
by Claude Lecouteux

Demons and Spirits of the Land
Ancestral Lore and Practices
by Claude Lecouteux

INNER TRADITIONS • BEAR & COMPANY
P.O. Box 388 • Rochester, VT 05767
1-800-246-8648
www.InnerTraditions.com

Or contact your local bookseller